Gatwick Park Days
A Gardening Memoir

Les Francis

Patchworks Publications

For Melanie and Emma

First published 2024
All content copyright © 2024 Les Francis
Copyright © 2006 Les Francis
Photo Credits: © 1996 – 2002 Les Francis

Les Francis asserts the moral right to be recognised
as the author of this work

Acknowledgements

Thanks to John, Works Manager at BUPA Gatwick Park Hospital, who hired me and permitted me free reign, pretty much, to develop the grounds and water features as I thought fit. His retirement was an end of an era moment for me.

Thanks to Brian, whose mantle I took on and whose good company I shared in the grounds for some six fine summers long.

Thanks to staff and patients alike whose kind comments of appreciation I received, unsolicited, by letter and by word of mouth.

Those Gatwick Park days were good old days, indeed. Well-spent, missed much and lamented more for their passing, they are a joy treasured yet for the memories they recall.

Little things, small and insignificant, trifling even, may conjure fond reminiscence. Others, singularly unique and striking, stand apart and come to mind to prompt a ready smile.

All are noteworthy and remarkable alike in their own right. Each, filed away, is a library to be plundered, ever a prize to seize upon for mention.

Contents

Gatwick Park Days – Tales, tall but true

1. Old Graylag — 7
2. Monsieur Le Fox — 23
3. No Smoke Without Fire! — 32
4. The Floating Island — 38
5. The Floating Island: Post Script — 56
6. The White Swan — 58
7. The Grand-Daddy Pike — 70
8. The Grand-Daddy Pike: Post Script — 89
9. The Garden Fox — 93
10. The Garden Fox Cub — 101
11. Another Rats Tale! — 107
12. The Great Flood — 118
13. The Final Curtain — 132

Notes & Anecdotes – Divers & Diverse

The Order of The Spade — 134
Garden Features — 135
'Upcycling' and Repurposing — 138
Listen to your Garden — 140
Of Remedies and the Remarkable — 145

List of Photographic Illustrations

The field outcrop — 149
The flood plain in flood — 149
The Duck House on the bank upon completion — 150
The Duck House settled on its raised piles — 150
The hedge laid with heel cuttings — 151
The hedge with stile constructed as a feature… — 151
The One Life Award — 152
The Award Ceremony — 152
Comments of appreciation, unsolicited… — 153
The floating island from the promenade — 154
The floating island from the far bank — 154
At the top of the drive – 'Ring out the old…' — 155
And – 'Ring in the new…' — 155
Crossing to the rustic bench in the pond precincts — 156
The bird table in the 'secret garden' — 156

Bringing on the seedlings and bedding	157
The grasscrete up to the 'secret garden'	157
The viewing area from the pond precincts	158
The pond precincts with the pair of Pedunculates	158
Carp water – "The pair of Pedunculates"	159
Carp water – The stream, culverted beneath	159
The Moorhen – "a loud and abrupt hiss…"	160
The Mallard – "a devoted but careless parent…"	160
The Salicifolia – "which I had intended to..."	161
Viewed from the drive. Viewed toward the drive	161
The front entrance	162
January snowscape	162
The "steps cut into the steep bank of the brook."	163
"… the stout boards that girded its width."	163
Stands of Purple Loosestrife and the Aruncas	164
The crossing that was well and truly buried…!	164
"My eyes perceived a sable form..."	165
"He stood there, calm as day, standing over..."	165
"A bridge of suitable structure was constructed..."	166
"Many crossings were added..."	166
From this, to this – "the project will design itself…"	167
"…forcing you to be resourceful..."	167
"Refurbish an old pot…"	168
"Knock together an eye-catching container…"	168
"Features may stand out..."	169
"The humble pebble or stone on the beach …"	169
"Take cuttings to increase your plant stock."	170
"The evidence that presented itself was…of galls."	170

GATWICK PARK DAYS: 1

Old Graylag

All winter long, Old Graylag stood, the stoic, solitary and alone upon the frozen pond. He could not fly away to balmier climes; he had to stick it out: his wings had been clipped; he could not fly.

It had been the intention of the clipping to keep him resident in the hospital grounds. Of course, that intent was meant to be a temporary affair only, a short term measure, an impediment to be imposed upon him for just sufficiently long enough that he may become acquainted and endeared with this, his planned summer residence, and so attached that he would want to return the following spring.

Unfortunately for the poor goose, the procedure had been over-thoroughly done; they had made a rather more than intended, permanent job of it. So, there he stood, desolate and alone, one leg tucked up inside beneath his downy jacket, in contemplative posture, an avian guru.

He yet had the use of his sea legs, but never more would those wings flap, take flight and bear him aloft on some updraught, up into the cloudy blue yonder. This was the hand he had been dealt. Still, he had dealt with it amiably enough, without apparent complaint.

This particular winter, however, had been more particularly harsh and severe and the welcoming beckon of sanctuary and safety upon the water had been snatched from him, encased beneath an unyielding crust of ice. He had lost even the use of his sea legs.

He had not even the solace of a mate for company. Her wings had been clipped also but had recovered and repaired and she had flown off to other parts to leave him to his lot, grounded, earthbound.

Having refound the use of her wings, she had circled round, once, twice, several times, calling out to him urgently, encouraging him to follow. He could not, of course, as much as he tried.

At first, he had run around and around, his wings all in a flap of fluster and frustrated effort to take to the air, in a state of utter and complete distress. As loud became the desperation of her summons, as desperate became his vain attempts to follow.

Finally, resigned – or reconciled to this unhappy state of affairs, or both – he stood watching her forlornly with those sad, unbelieving eyes of his as, one last time, exasperated perhaps, failing to understand his predicament, she flew off, never to return.

Old Graylag adapted. He played the cards he had been dealt. He would not permit his circumstance to dispirit or discourage him in his daily life. He had little choice in the matter after all, but perhaps it is as Lawrence baldly observed: "I never saw a wild thing sorry for itself..." for, without whinge or whimper or any complaint of any kind, or none that was apparent in any way, Old Graylag had just got on with it and made the best of what he had.

Seasons passed. Old Graylag had adopted and been adopted by the resident Mallards and their extended families. The Moorhens, too, had taken a shine to him. He had become quite a character had Old Graylag, a celebrity both among his avian kind and the keen human observer of their daily antics. And so did this pleasant state of affairs continue for some several years.

During this while, it was the hospital's policy to feed the resident water fowl with a daily ration of grain. Ever the gentleman that he was, the old goose would politely take his turn to scoop up his appropriate share of the nutritious feed, along with the shy Moorhens who would dart in and out at first glimpse of an opening. Not all, however, were as unobtrusive, unassuming or shy.

Brash, not thoughtless but without thought for their fowlkind, the Mallards, would make a disorderly charge for the various deposited piles and, with swaggering gait, dig straight in with a will and gusto! It was in their character, I suppose, so to do. Likewise, they were not uncaring but, rather, careless parents. This, also, was their character.

They would fuss and bother their little broods to keep up and summon them sharply to return to their side should they wander – as they would. Invariably, however, they would lose one or two of their fluffy offspring every few days – perhaps to the pool, perhaps to the Pike, eventually reducing their number to just a pair or just a solitary one!

Old Graylag, by contrast, would have made a superb parent, had circumstance favoured him differently. He was both mother-clucking hen and – being a head and a long goose-neck above all the rest – soldier and sentry, protecting his adopted charges.

There was chicken-wire set in place about the pond enclosure at that time. This was intended to serve the dual purpose of containment of the inmates to the pond precincts and the exclusion of predators from them. An electrified barrier consisting of a tripwire had been installed also and this served as an additional line of defence and deterrent.

This 'disincentive', a further and supplementary hurdle, 'raised the bar' to the local vulpine gentry – or, leastwise, provided greater challenge for them sufficient, it was hoped, to discourage and dissuade that opportunist criminal company from any attempt to gain an entry! As things turned out, however, the wire mesh proved to be more in the manner of a hazard to those it was intended to protect, more a Maginot line, than a line of defence.

The Scottish Bard it was who said of the best laid plans of mice and men that they oft 'gang a-gley' and, oft, they do and in a manner not at all intended nor, indeed, at all contemplated by anyone's wildest imaginings and certainly not those of the ones who make them. And this was the way it panned out and in a most unexpected way.

It had been just another morning, one of many. All was proceeding just as it always did. The feed had just been deposited in its various piles along and about the enclosure in order to provide as little reason for disagreement and squabble as possible – not at all that this intent was sufficient

Gatwick Park Days - *A Gardening Memoir*

for purpose. All was, in other words, utter fowlish confusion and mayhem!

The ducklings, for their part, for the moment left to their own devices, scurried hither and thither, thoroughly enjoying the havoc and chaos of the proceedings! And thus did this cacophonous but happy state of affairs continue for some few minutes, until a great commotion erupted.

Old graylag stood at sentry call, his long neck craned forward, head held high, eyes all intent, baying at the scudding clouds skating past overhead in a Fastnet flotilla all their own! All called to attend the breakfast spectacular that morning did marvel and remark upon this extraordinary performance as the sight of the old fellow making such uproar and disturbance drew everyone's notice.

Such lively trepidation it was that everyone's focus was captured. One and all, the various matinee promenaders were brought to a halt. Those who had parked themselves leisurely on the bench to witness the daily circus were brought in turn, in an abrupt start, to their feet. All gazed at the fellow in astonishment. Whatever could be the matter that appeared to cause such alarm?

An Atlantic-bound liner roared a majestic and loud farewell to the tree-topped Gatwick skyline, then sailed silently aloft flanked by marbled clouds clumped in tall chimneys. Far off, a dog's bark, terse and sharp, carried on the wind, intervened. Unheard and disregarded, the canine protest faded into the distance with the jumbo and its human cargo, but the old goose did not let up once and continued to make a scene.

Bill gaped wider than a Pike's gutting maw, Old Graylag sounded forth his claxon call. Warning alarm, a call to arms or a cry for assistance; whichever, what was it, - or none of these? Whatever was the cause of his agitated state, becoming more and more dire and more urgent by the moment?

There seemed no apparent answer or resolution to these questions, now matters of open debate amongst the gathering congregation of those called present by the racket to bear witness. All pondered this odd spectacle most readily in puzzlement and concern.

Everyone, all and sundry, struck by the mystery of it all, looked about them for some cause, some explanation for this unseemly disruption of the proceedings and this most anomalous behaviour. Old Graylag, for his part, his usually dignified demean banished to some dark and distant nether region, merely persisted more insistently and more readily and with more determination!

Gatwick Park Days - *A Gardening Memoir*

The Avian School of Comportment and Etiquette for Young Gentle-geese, which Old Graylag must surely have attended and graduated from with first degree honours, so fine and well-mannered typically and usually was his behaviour in all other circumstance, would never have approved! All began to conjecture and surmise on his untypical outburst.

Was there a storm brewing, some asked? A fox, another asserted with confidence! - At this late hour of the morning? This would require more close attention and investigation, clearly; and, as the discussion proceeded, it became obvious that this duty would fall to me, as assigned hospital functionary in this department, to look into the matter more closely.

I descended the steps cut into the steep bank of the brook and crossed by the stout boards that girded its width. As I approached him, Old Graylag did not calm one bit, as I thought he might have done, but carried on unremittingly. In fact, his cry became all the louder, the more insistent at my approach, as if to hasten me on.

He did not move, but maintained his ground, and I became all the more concerned and curious about whatever it could be that so disturbed him. As I deftly reached his position and came alongside him, I could not have imagined, not ever, what there befell my eyes.

Gatwick Park Days - *A Gardening Memoir*

A clutch of downy little fellows, ducklings, four or five in number, not more than two fortnights old, had entangled themselves, or become so entangled, in the chicken-wire that lined and defined the bank-side. The wire mesh cordon descended, top to bottom, down into the cloudy depths and there they struggled to get free, their efforts unproductive, futile and to no avail.

Old Graylag spread his wings as if to indicate them to me, as if I had not already seen them for myself and become aware of the scrape they had gotten themselves into. The mesh had become detached and they sat thrashing about, flapping flightless wings, trapped between the bank and the wire above the drab and dingy murk of the watery swirl beneath.

Old Graylag threw me a glance, a frantic glare, urging me on to do something, anything at all that might remedy the situation. Helpless to achieve any outcome himself his attention returned once more to their plight. His apparent confidence in my ability to intervene where he could not; to come to their assistance to facilitate for them a release from their unfortunate predicament: this humbled me profoundly.

The old goose looked at me again, askance, intent upon the plight of the wayward fledglings. He flapped his wings impatiently and with urgent trepidation, insistent that I should formulate some means of escape for them. His estimation of my abilities was fast failing and, obviously, shaken! I would have to act quickly if I was to bring about some favourable outcome to the circumstance and restore his apparent unerring faith in humankind.

I knelt; reached down and shook the wire. The ducklings tumbled free into the brook; scampered, scattered, splashed through the ragged tangle of Burr Reed and Plantain, then up into the tall, lanky spikes of Willow Herb and Loosestrife where they hid themselves, in fear or shame, I know not which!

Old Graylag tossed his head loftily; ceased his claxon call abruptly. I confess it impressed me greatly how quickly was restored his calm. All semblance of alarm faded and, with a shuffling gait, his duty done, he rejoined the mayhem of Mallards arguing over the pyramids of grain.

The gallimaufrous racket of the assembled melange subsided. The gravitas of his presence was it, or his forcefulness of purpose, his stature perhaps, that appeared to police or to restrain them? Whichever it was, as he proceeded to thread his way amongst them, their mannerless ebullience, their unseemly and extreme over-zealousness, seemed to subside and so did the shambles return to order and their rowdy, indecorous behaviour moderated accordingly.

Gatwick Park Days - *A Gardening Memoir*

Careless parents, indeed, they were, and clueless. The Mallards had not even noticed the almost dire and near calamitous scrape their infant charges had gotten themselves into! There was no medal to afford him but our admiration for his selfless concern, his dedication of purpose; but he appeared indifferent to praise or the lack of it in any case and, content with the outcome, had rejoined the feast.

No thanks were there for him amongst the avian ranks, not even acknowledgement. Their focus had been set upon the banquet before them anyhow The unsung hero of the hour, he appeared to care little or not of that either and bore the award we had conferred upon him, such as it was, with apparent modesty and diffidence. Unaware, if that he was and may well have been, he must surely have noted what followed, however.

I stood there for some few brief moments, observing the scene, when a further commotion erupted to disturb my quiet repose. Applause arose along the bank from among the band of watchers of the fowlish drama that had unfolded: but a brief applause but acknowledgement, still, such that it was.

If this was for me or for Old Graylag, or for us all as actors participant in the unscripted drama and spectacle, I cannot say or be certain. I cannot be sure, but my applause, my admiration, my praise, was solidly, unarguably reserved for the stout-hearted gallant.

Had the fellow taken note or oblivious was he of this, also? He made no acknowledgement that I could discern. No matter, for he was justly rewarded with the feast before him: a pile of grain that, by happenstance or circumstance in all the squabbling that had proceeded, appeared to have been overlooked by his fellows and into which he scooped with most joyful gusto!

Times passed, as times must. Change comes. The old regime gives way to the new. The changes were rung and the bell ringers called a different tune. Savings were called for. The new had assumed its own priorities and the grain ration was, alas, not one of them. When all is said and done, even a minuscule saving may, perhaps, weighed in the balance, just tip the scales sufficiently to balance the outgoings!

When purse strings are tightened choices must be made. When penury knocks at the door, deliberation reigns in any incautious extravagance and prudence is sweet meat to swallow to bitter rancour born of reckless profligacy. Eitherwise, for what reason, whether diligent deliberation or departmental politics, hospitality was lavished no longer in the form of luncheon for our avian guests. In the accountant's reckoning, at least, this was to be a removable feast!

Gatwick Park, henceforward, would play host no longer to such numbers, resident or migrant, as previously it did and our avian guest list declined. With no show to put on at the amphitheatre, the attendant numbers of spectators also declined. The audience appeared to lose the interest they had once displayed with such persistent reliability and were called no more to take a morning promenade along the bank for that purpose.

Chicks and ducks and geese all scurried! With no 'king's shilling' to retain their loyalty - their 'tipple' withdrawn - the water fowl population slowly but surely dwindled to a bare fraction of what had once been.

A band of vagrant Canadas continued to fly in to deposit a pair of their number with us. These happily summered through, still content with what the pond precincts could provide, and would then depart to seek winter quarters with their kin and kind elsewhere.

Whilst one Moorhen pair remained ever faithful, unperturbed seemingly and indifferent, tolerating this downgrade of their prior five-star lifestyle, others of their feathered kind were not so forgiving. Of the avian populace that remained, the Mallard contingent deserted us like a trickle until we were left with but a pair of ducks and their attendant suitors.

So, here now he stood, surveying the bleak and frozen pond. Old Graylag, the cold warrior, standing sentry, alone and forgotten like all old soldiers, was reliant alone on morsels of bread that were tossed to him that were not stolen by scavenging gulls.

Even these few Mallards that remained now preferred and chose to winter at the broader lake waters provided by Riverside, adjacent the Gatwick Stream. They had rejoined their cousins and moved on to those more open stretches, less sheltered, but less likely to freeze over as had our pond.

All winter long, the old fellow braved it out, not entirely on his own but still alone. The Moorhen pair remained, their Moor-chicks having long flown the nest to seek their own fortunes elsewhere, but these were private creatures and kept their own company.

They would venture out briefly and on occasion, but preferred to remain reclusive. Amongst the dead spikes of reed mace and rushes, hidden from view, they were a present if not visible company for Old Graylag, at least, and surely a comfort that he was not entirely alone.

Gatwick Park Days - *A Gardening Memoir*

Then, one cold, January day, he was gone. How I cannot say. There was not a sign of him, not anywhere. There was no indication of struggle, no trace of any mortal remains. I searched and searched about the grounds and not a sign of him could I find. No corpse, no feather, ruffled or bloodied was there. No 'Campden Wonder' this: he was truly gone!

He could not have flown off! Neither would he have feasibly wandered far from the protective confines of the pond precincts. This was his universe; this was all he had ever known since the day, long time ago, they had brought him here and performed the ill-fated clipping of his wings.

Had a fox, indeed, taken him? It was possible if, old and feeble, he was unable to resist and put up a last fight to save himself; perhaps, then, no evidence would have been left of the deed! Could that be so?

Had he just succumbed to the cold, inclement conditions that had persisted all winter through? Had he found somewhere safe, secluded, as wild creatures do, to just curl up in - and die?

Had some guardian angel of the avian kind, compassionate, merciful, come down to retrieve his broken, frail and fragile physical form and restored his wings to soar aloft once more and grace the sky of some glorious avian heaven?

Gatwick Park Days - *A Gardening Memoir*

I do declare, I shall never know. I do confess, though, however fanciful that may seem, I would rather it were the latter.

GATWICK PARK DAYS: 2

Monsieur Le Fox

The news had come as something of a shock. I had been advised by someone out walking their dog – one of our daily throng of many visitors – that, upon the little chap's perambulations about our extensive grounds, they had come upon a dead fox. I went to investigate, as I had been informed, down by the pool. I sought him out and there he lay, not but a couple of metres from where I had seen him the day previously. His carcase was in a running pose, already stiff. Stock still, like a corpse myself, I stood momentarily to take it in. An observer of myself, moved but unmoving, shock-still I stood and numbed by the sight of him.

I confess, I had half-expected this what here befell my gaze but, even so, the sight of him there served only to reinforce the sense of utter disbelief I felt; of loss to see the old fellow, this long-time acquaintance, in his sad and tragic demise. A committed resolve took hold of me then. I shook off the numbness that had stilled me like a stone statue to the spot and, trekking back toward the hut, nodding a grim and certain acknowledgement to the man and his dog, still

Gatwick Park Days - *A Gardening Memoir*

hunting scents across the way, I retrieved a spade from the wheelbarrow I had left parked at the head of the culvert.

It was a solemn task I set myself to undertake then but, determinedly, I set to work to carry it through. I intended to lay him to rest just there, by the pool. It seemed, in some way that I cannot explain, fitting that this should be his last and final resting place, amongst the pussy willows that had provided a canopy of shade for him in life upon such pleasant mornings as this, by the reedy edge of the pool, in these such pleasant surrounds I know, for a surety, he must have loved and appreciated as much as did I.

I set to work with a will and excavated a hole of sufficient volume and dimension, not merely to accommodate his not insubstantial remains, but that he might lie there undisturbed, safe from scrutiny, concealed quite from the delving eye, from the over-curious and the ill-intended. The task took up most of my morning. To complete the interment, I scattered a covering of reeds and rushes and stipa fronds to camouflage the area as best I could so that no passing forager might be any the wiser.

We had first made acquaintance some two or three years before. At least, that was our first 'close encounter' so to speak. I had become and been made aware of his presence over quite some period of time. The fox is a determined creature of habit and there were the tell-tale signs: the well-worn track, for instance, which followed the line of Leylandii along the western perimeter of the hospital grounds. Other signs besides there were as well.

The fox will follow his route faithfully on his nightly rounds and no impediment will bar him from it. Our fox had even burrowed a way beneath the boundary fence to gain access to the rear garden of the bungalow that sat at the top of the drive. The alternative would have been to advance a little further along the fence line and then to proceed along the drive itself. That would not have been sufficiently private for his nature or his liking, however.

'Brookdale' had once been an adjunct medical centre for the hospital proper; no more, and the bungalow had since been turned over to a storage facility for medical records. The gardens, front and back, had still to be maintained, however, and so it was, out of interest, curiosity, to discourage the impudent creature from this brash, uncaring, thoughtless intrusion that quite ruined the lawn aspect, I had raked the excavated earth back into place and, thus, blocked his means of entry. Who am I fooling, only myself, not you, the reader, surely? Was it not the sheer devilment of it I did it, to see what he would do?

Gatwick Park Days - *A Gardening Memoir*

Stubborn, resolute fellow he was, but would this ploy deter him quite so easily?

I would dearly have loved to have seen the look on the rascal's face when he discovered my little exercise – or prank was it? – but that could not be. I left work reluctantly that day, aching to be back in the morning to see how he had reacted to it. Had he been foiled; had he found another way around? I pictured him, the look of utter dumbfoundment fresh upon his face, sniffing here, there. No, not at all, not a bit of it! Next day, all was back as it had been before I undertook my mischief. The fence had been neatly tunnelled once more, in exactly the place he had excavated previously. A determined and tenacious fellow, indeed, he was!

The town fox is bolder than his country counterpart. This fellow was not quite either, residing neither in rural nor urban domain, but rather more, but not quite, suburban environs. His nature, accordingly, was neither that of the one nor the other, but retaining some of the timidity and timorousness of his country cousin. My work about the grounds and his passage through them, however, made it inevitable, I suppose, that our paths should cross eventually; and so it was, one day, they did! I shall return, therefore, to this first encounter – 'in the flesh' as it were.

Gatwick Park Days - *A Gardening Memoir*

It was one morning, early, at the point where the stream gains entry to the site by way of a culvert sitting on the western boundary line. Where I had set stones across for a weir and steps down to it to ford the brook, he came bounding up, a big town fox – or suburban fox but still of substantial propertion! Then, freeze-framed, as was I, not two metres apart, we stood: he, beautiful, proud, haughty; I, curious, stunned, in silent awe. A second, two, and he started; turned abruptly, and retraced his steps down across the brook and up the other side. Gone!

It was approaching Christmas that same year when he took the goose: a big old Canada gander, orphaning a family of three cumbersome goose-chicks. It was the first and last clutch of goslings a pair of Canadas had stayed to rear. Previously, they had visited, overstayed briefly to taste of what delights the grounds had to offer, and then flown on to more tempting venues – or those more suitable, perhaps, to the rearing of their offspring. While our grounds were a delight in themselves, there were more open stretches of water locally, adjacent to the Gatwick Stream for instance, and these had been given obvious preference to our more modest-sized pool. That year, our delights had, evidently, proved too much of a delight to resist and, in succumbing to this temptation, the old gander had met his nemesis in Monsieur Le Fox!

He had died protecting them, I am sure, - the goose and her attendant gaggle. He had died the glorious death; made the beautiful sacrifice. Carried off, taken to stock Monsieur Le Fox's Christmas larder, he was the prize item, the main course, no doubt, for his Christmas fayre! All that was left - the only evidence of the deed - was the scattered disarray of feathers which were, everywhere, strewn across the footpath and into the shrubbery borders. During the night, there had been quite a something and a muchness of a terrible commotion. A great struggle had quite evidently taken place, as those who were awoken from their slumbers all later concurred and the crime scene so attested. There had been a wailing and a squealing that would have put a whole coddle of banshees to shame!

Monsieur Le Fox had imprinted his mark indelibly upon us all upon that night of infamy! Those who were previously aware of his traffic through the grounds were now only too alert to his presence. He and his dastardly deed became all the talk for some few weeks, well into the new year when, after much time and at much effort, the lone widow goose managed finally to coax her brood into the air, having convinced them that they could, indeed, fly as well as swim! Talk of the crime diminished after that into small talk and then dissipated altogether as new topics of conversation arose amongst the tattletales, - as they do seem so to do.

Gatwick Park Days - *A Gardening Memoir*

As for the Canadas, they continued with their vernal visitations, announcing themselves with a great fanfare of pomp and circumstance. A flotilla of them, or squadron if you will, would sail into the wind and land on the pond. Always seven of them there were, without fail or fall through. A magnificent seven, they would then pamper and cosset themselves with whatever facilities were available for the taking before depositing two of their number on site and the remaining five setting sail upon their skyward journey once again. Lurching, tottering, their great bulk gaining speed and height, and then gracefully taking wing, they circled, honking and hooting their farewells before departing.

Yes, the goose had found herself another gander, or I assume that to be so, else this was a different pair altogether for the band had not depleted any in number! - Never more, however, did this pair who chose to remain overstay to nest and attend to the business of raising another brood. Our port of call had, quite evidently, earned a not undeservedly bad reputation amongst their happy band! So, we would have their company for awhile, then, having tired of whatever comforts we had to offer and taken their fill - ever come Eastertide - they would be off and gone, and sail into the sun upon their way. Every year but one did they, when I undertook the making of a floating island!

Gatwick Park Days - *A Gardening Memoir*

And Monsieur le Fox? It was on a Thursday, one late October afternoon, fast approaching eventide; the date is forever book-marked in the diary of my mind. The 24^h October 2002 it was, and I spied the fellow lying at the pool's edge on the far side from my standpoint. He had his back to me. I was not downwind, I made no attempt to disguise my approach, yet he paid me no heed as I advanced and came within ten metres of him. Had he not taken my scent, had he not heard my approach? I called out to him several times, his only acknowledgement an eventual sidewise glance of the head! And there he sat, in a beacon of sunshine arcing through the Salix boughs, uncaring of my presence, unperturbed by my brash intrusion upon his reverie.

Absorbed totally, I idled there for some long while and, with or without his permission but, surely, with his certain acquiescence, shared his company, took delight in the pleasant aspect, as did he, or so it did appear. The several and various tasks I had set myself from the morning were set aside, went by the board. So taken was I, so entranced in our mutual vigil, that it was only with some great effort of determination that I dragged myself back to my responsibilities. I left him there, sunning himself as I thought. I could not have been more wrong.

The following day, not five metres from where I had spied him at the pool's edge, he lay dead.

Gatwick Park Days - *A Gardening Memoir*

From his running pose, I could tell he had set out with some intent, some great purpose of mind. Perhaps, the old vagabond's heart had finally given out and brought him crumbling to his knees. I cannot say.

It's said by some, the sagacious the erudite and the worldly wise, that something of yourself brushes off onto others and that something of them brushes off onto you. Such a melancholy snatched at my soul then that I think a piece of me must have brushed off onto him and died there with him. If that is true, though – what these wizens say – then something of him lives on in me, for it seems that I carry his memory with me always.

GATWICK PARK DAYS: 3

No Smoke Without Fire!

It was a mid-week morning when the fire alarm reached my ears a full half-way up the drive, a claxon call commanding my attention. The sounders were unremitting, unrelenting in their summons. Attentively and dutifully, I halted my work schedule and looked down toward the hospital building for sign of activity. No-one appeared at all phased and I stood on the small meadow adjacent the car park, utterly bemused by the scene.

There was no orderly rush to evacuate, as there might be reasonably expected. The reception doors continued to part and swallow up the day's intake of customers and visitors. Everyone just continued going about their daily business, all happily, blissfully ignoring this blatant intrusion upon the orderly doings of the day. No smoke without fire, they say, but there was none.

Was that the way of it that there was none who appeared at all perturbed by the certain and incessant call to take action? Was it that all were confident that someone else would be or was attending to the summons? Surely, that may well *have been the case: when car alarms sound out their mayday distress calls, as not so infrequently they do, their hue and cry goes mostly ignored and not attended to. There is never exclamation or outcry at anyone's presence in the vicinity of any protesting vehicle, who might just as well be an offending and potential carjacker or car cracksman as being assumed to be the car's keeper!*

Still the fire precautions have to be followed and so they had been. It was a cascade system that was adhered to religiously. It was the kitchen again. Another false alarm, I surmised; or, most likely, that was the case! Who was the culprit and what was the cause? Which was it: an over-sensitive or temperamental detector or an overdone main off the carte du jour done too many turns? I cannot say, but it was a sure-fire certainty it was one or other of them.

That is not to cast aspersions on the integrity of the staff restaurant; no, not at all. The restaurant - yes, restaurant - did a fine cuisine. The chef took great pride in turning out a range of choice dishes that would have been the pride and envy of the best haute cuisine on the high street and to the satisfaction of the most discerning epicure or gourmet grande. It was via this reliable source I first learned the difference between the venerable Cottage Pie and the humble Shepherd's Pie. The former was made, originally, with the fresh ingredients; the latter was made with the leftovers - as was Bubble and Squeak!

I had been informed, as if by way of some verification or assurance of his quite apparent and obvious competence as a cordon bleu, that he had acquired a guest house locally, one of the many that jostled here for business; one among the many local hotels that thronged the locale, both small and large, and bed-and-breakfasts that served the airport. This became an additional commitment to him which, very soon, became a priority; one which would come to demand his focus eventually, to forsake us entirely in order to devote his full time and best efforts to.

The loud, incessant, jarring clang fell silent. The fire station, conveniently, was not far up the road and, already, the familiar 'nee naw' of a siren could be heard above the bustle of the scene beset before me. Then, there was a great roar as the fire engine turned into the drive, up by the road, and heaved its way down toward the hospital. The fire brigade was attending! Ah, who remembers, long back in the day, when every emergency service vehicle was equipped, not with a horn or a siren or whatever, but a bell? The familiar clang and clapper of the bells slowly disappeared from our streets not long after we signed up to the Common Market and even ditched our good old pounds, shillings and pence!

Gatwick Park Days - *A Gardening Memoir*

The fire alarm was linked in by some means or other to the fire station. The cascade would have required the 'appointed person' to have already been on the phone to alert or inform the fire service whichever way it was and, clearly, from the leisurely pace at which the fire tender jaunted down the drive it would have been a certain bet to say it was a false alarm. They would, in any case, be required to attend, if just to satisfy themselves that all was safe and sound, and here they were!

Just then, on cue, and as if to salute their arrival but not quite satisfied that its duty, done, had been sufficiently acknowledged, the alarm gave one last burst and dropped again into a great hush. The daily comings and goings, still unabashed by any failure to respond, merely continued to proceed as though nothing of any account had happened at all. There was none to blink or bat an eyelid when the big red fire engine rolled past the staff car park, the faces of the fire crew beaming from the cab. None raised an eye as they rolled past the visitor's car park and approached the small bridge that crossed the stream and where they drew to an abrupt halt... Then, a murmur and a hum of amusement arose in quite a disorderly commotion!

Heads were turned; eyes were fixed; everyone's attention was caught by such a sight, it was truly a sight to see. Everyone's interest was drawn to the

Gatwick Park Days - *A Gardening Memoir*

little procession that was approaching the road in such a haste, intent, oblivious to everyone and everything around as a fat, squat Mallard fussed and flapped and waddled and toddled and shuffled, looking back upon herself to check and chastise and make reprimand with her charges - a queue of noisy duck-chicks, following behind!

The disorderly train trooped at her instruction, out across the footpath, straight into the road, directly in front of the big red fire engine, blocking its path, that it could do small else than shudder to a halt! Whither bound were they with such a sense of purpose and urgency I could not think or guess or possibly say without doubt or with any reasonable certainty. Bound for some nearby riverside caravanserai were they that had found favour amongst her kind? The firemen all peered down from out their cab in bewildered bemusement, a beam of merriment adorning each astonished countenance!

With a waddle and a quack, the fat, squat Mallard and her long train of noisy duck-chicks sauntered on across the roadway directly in front of the huge vehicle, unaware totally or ignorant of the threat it might have posed. Cosseting her retinue to heed and follow her instruction, she urged them on. It was, indeed, a sight to see and all gave pause to take a moment out their day to see it!

Gatwick Park Days - *A Gardening Memoir*

The vehicle brought thus to a jolty standstill, they safely reached the other side. With a little hop, a skip and a jump, they mounted the kerb and lumbered onto the small meadow where I yet stood agape at it all. The comedy of it could not have been contrived; it would surely have been considered as so unlikely to occur, but occur it did and we all, privileged few, had been witness to it. They hurried past me on their way and disappeared into the brush along by the boundary fence.

All woke abruptly from the momentary thrall that had been cast upon us and continued on about our day. The big red fire engine awoke, too, with a roar and a shudder and sloped off toward the building where it came to a halt by the reception. Then, with great aplomb, out trooped the firemen, all dressed in their finery of new brown fatigues. The once familiar blue uniform was long consigned to the past, just as has that of ambulance personnel, now all dressed in green! Times change so and the familiar is discarded with apparent disdain.

GATWICK PARK DAYS: 4

The Floating Island

I had taken it upon myself to over-winter my time with the task of creating a second, smaller pond in the shallows upstream adjacent the main pond feature. The seasonal lull in the necessity of mowing allowed me the time freed up from this busy summer schedule of edging and lawn manicure, maintaining field and meadow, and attending to beds, baskets and borders to accomplish the task and I set about it with a purpose and zeal.

These shallows were largely a broad bog-land of reed mace and rushes and I used the long hook that had been fashioned from a fork and a long pole of metal conduit to dredge the brook to drag these out and form a serpentine isthmus to mark the new pond's edge.

The task was most laborious but equally satisfying and, as the undertaking progressed throughout the shortening autumn days that ensued, the work slowly took shape and was most impressive in its resulting outcome. I was not solely employed in this, of course, as the seasonal callings also demanded attention to take up my time.

Trees shed their growth all through the year but autumn-time it is the mantle of growth becomes, not a shed, but a great dump to clear and tidy. It is another fine time of the year to appreciate the tans and rustic browns and golden tones that adorn them. It was a bright, warm day that found me round from the rear of the building to the front. The sun was slung low in the sky, as it is as the year moves to its close, and glanced my face most welcomingly, as though it were a caress.

It was a most pleasing sensation, indeed, and a most pleasant aspect that presented itself to me as I turned the corner. The broad lawn, newly planted with clumps of shrubs and cuttings I had gleaned from about the grounds spread before me. The paved footpath wound its way off toward the bank. Everything was bathed in a warm glow, or so it did appear to my eyes. The scene embraced me utterly. Then, the most remarkable thing: A great 'dump' of leaves fell – floated! – from the great mantle of the pair of Pedunculates that skirted the bend in the brook and provided cover for the carp and tench that darted there.

I am sure it was only for but brief minutes but I stood there, transfixed, for what seemed like hours. There was not a breath of wind that took them down but down they came, floating like a shower of confetti at a celebration of union. Perhaps, that's what it was I was witness to: a sacred marriage, an autumnal rite, a festival of earth and sky all set to the unorchestrated impromptu of a blackbird warbling from the treetop!

It was not just the sun was warm: the light itself it bathed that gay and pleasant afternoon with touched my face and I felt myself aglow in its embrace! Yes! It was a union, officiated by the sun, gazing fondly down upon this, his happy congregation! I proceeded on my way through the rain of confetti and felt a oneness, a union with the world.

Later that afternoon, I was presented with an idea by the Works Manager that took me pleasantly by surprise at its prospect and challenge. He had come upon a report of conservationists who had constructed a floating island, no less, out on some estuary, and proposed it as a suggestion for my undertaking! He handed me some papers – photocopies he had made containing the report. I received them happily, enthused at the thought of such a commission being served up to me!

I pondered on it long all that evening, such that, upon the following day, I had some good idea in my head on how to proceed. It was just the barebones account I had; no plans were included for its construction. It was intended for sea birds so, thinking an adaptation of some sort may be in order to accommodate their nature, I set out first to build a little house to sit upon the island – a duck house – which I thought might also make an attractive and useful addition!

There were always odd bits of timber around – off-cuts and so on – and it wasn't long before I had knocked together a serviceable-looking and respectable likeness of one. There was a fair weight to it that inclined me to ponder, would it capsize the island once I got it afloat. No matter for the moment, I proceeded to lug it onto the trailer and drive it across to the pond side where it sat ready, a curiosity for all to ponder!

Some few days passed before the project could be resumed. I needed pallets for a platform or raft to float the island on. There were always a good many to be found in the skip and I hauled four of them on the trailer over to the pond precinct. Next, I hunted about for rope with which to lash them together. There was a huge reel of 3-strand nylon rope in the workshop and I borrowed this for the purpose. All was looking good and sound as I deliberated then on what next to proceed with.

On the undertaking in the estuary, they had used substantial, purpose-built floats to serve their island buoyancy and I wondered what could be

Gatwick Park Days - *A Gardening Memoir*

provided for this. What was there that I had at my disposal? My efforts were humble and meagre by comparison to theirs and it came to me that, if there might be any available that they could spare, the empty oil drums from the kitchen might well suffice to launch the project upon the pond.

The waste oil was collected and recycled using the empty drums for its removal. There were always some spare, though, and I enquired at the kitchen if I might take some. The screw-top lids were airtight and, so I thought, would likewise be watertight. These were provided to me willingly. They had been flushed out and so would, surely, create no issues of pollution in either pond or watercourse.

Another trip over to the skip provided timber to construct a skirting to contain the drums. This was attached around the platform to prevent their escape and the rope employed to secure them in place. All was going well. The idea had been floated to me and the island, now taking form, would soon be floating on the pond!

The days that followed were again taken up by an assortment of seasonal and essential tasks and so further progress was at a halt. The platform sat there at the waterside, alone and unattended apart from the inquisitive Mallards hopping on and off this odd curiosity in their midst. The

Gatwick Park Days - *A Gardening Memoir*

more astute and discerning Moorhens afforded it not even a disdainful glance! They appeared oblivious absolutely, as if unaware of its presence, and continued about their business, foraging along the bank and investigating the reed mace and rushes about the pond's rim. They were not at all impressed or otherwise, in anywise, perturbed by it. It was not worthy of their attention.

I came back to it at the end of the week with fresh ideas on how to proceed. The bare boards of it had to be clothed in some manner with a covering of sorts of plants and a strata of soil to support them. What better than that already to hand - and the most appropriate: to make use of the native growth about the pond; and so I did proceed.

There was turf aplenty to be had and I cut this in manageable slices or, rather, as it was wont to detach itself from its anchorage, and carpeted the bare boards of the platform, permitting it to overhang the edge to hide the skirting. There was now quite a weight to it and I had to consider a launch upon the pond before continuing further to dress its precinct with a hide or two of tall stipa and rush to give it a more natural appearance.

The launch was undertaken with greater effort than I had imagined it might. The bulk did not appear that substantial but it was deceptive. I used the long pole of the dredging hook to lever it in shifts and shoves into the water. Shift it did and shoved and slid into the shallows with a splash. It was afloat! Relieved, I sighed a sigh of much satisfaction and self-congratulation.

It was then that the decision had to be made, whether to sit the duck house aboard. Would it look at home there, in any case, or would it look out of place? Catastrophe! The decision was made for me. One of the drums came adrift and the island lurched for a moment before bobbing and settling back into position. I heaved on the tether of rope I had secured to it to prevent it sailing off on some mission of its own hunch or inkling and it returned to a rest at the water-edge.

The loose drum sat there, mocking me that it had escaped, still secured by an unfastened knot of rope, but threatening to break free at any moment. I hooked it back in to prevent such an occurrence but I was still presented with the problem of how to return it to its original purpose. In ponderous thought, I donned the waders to step out into the shallows for the undertaking.

Easy, you might imagine. Not so! It's as hard, if not harder, to force an empty drum down into the drink as it is to lift a full drum off the solid ground! Furthermore, it had to be pushed down sufficiently to get it back beneath the skirt. With every effort and each heave-ho to get the drum down and under, it would force itself back against my huddling, flailing arms. I was threshing around and achieving nothing except the futile expenditure of my energy.

It was then I determined to make some other use of the duck house. The feasibility of setting it in place was a formidable proposition. Making all secure, I left the task to its devices to give it some further thought. There was other work to attend to about the grounds, in any case. The hedge-trimming had to be completed along the drive and this occupied my time for the rest of the day and the day following.

Garbed in my waders, I stood once more at the water's edge, the awaiting task confronting me. I had resolved to gird the raft with the coil of rope, over and beneath it. A sufficient length pulled from the underside was then secured to the wayward drum, binding it round several times to contain it. With each shove and push down into the water, I heaved on the other end of the rope to stop the drum from bobbing back up again, undoing all the effort spent on getting it down into the drink. It proved a Herculean task but, with one last heave-ho and shove, I succeeded in getting the errant back under the skirt and back into position.

The island lurched and bounced back with a jolt!

It looked much happier for the regained support the drum provided. With relief, I went on the hunt to unearth and pull some stipa and other suitable growth I could provide for a hide or two and, from an aesthetic point of view, to give it as natural an appearance I could and make the island as an attractive a feature as I might. The dredging fork was a most handy tool for this purpose and it heaved the grasses from their purchase with ease, or so it felt after the telling effort spent already in returning the drum to its purpose.

I looked at the isle with as creative an eye as I could muster to bed the plants in and, in the space of a short while, it began to have the natural look and appearance intended. Happy at last with the effort, the time had come to set sail and send it on its maiden voyage – the one and only journey I intended it to make, across to the centre of the pond.

The send-off was a quiet affair; there was no jubilant crowd as you would expect to send off an ocean liner! No, nothing as grand as that; I had an audience of just one Moorhen and a waddling and curious Mallard! I secured the remainder of the coil of rope and gave the raft, all dressed now in its finery of green growth, a final push off from the water's edge with the long pole of the dredging fork. It settled some ten foot or so off from me in the deep.

Gatwick Park Days - *A Gardening Memoir*

To provide a mooring, I sank a half-round stake into the shallows this side and, another, on the far side of the pond. A fisherman's knot to tie the rope to its tether supplied not only effective mooring but a nice look at the end of it. The only remaining task before me was to get the little island out to the centre.

The other mooring rope had to be weaved the water-side of all the pond-side growth - willows and all - around to the far side. This was not a simple undertaking, complicated by the random and careless boughs overhanging and dipping into the drink. As I proceeded, the unavoidable tugging on the rope to avoid the outgrowth actually enabled my efforts to haul the island on its plotted course and - finally - it did begin to look like the floating island that had been envisaged!

This other end of rope was secured with a bowline knot such that sailors use to attach a halyard. It would serve purpose to loop over the stake to afford effective mooring but could be removed quickly and easily to pull the island back to shore should that become necessary. The slack was taken up and all was finally shipshape and Bristol fashion! It was truly a floating island looking as if it grew there. The proof of the pudding would be in the eating, though. How would our discerning fowlish community, resident and migrant, take to it?

Imperceptibly, the autumn days grew shorter, the evenings drew in and winter was soon upon us. The Moorhens scooted on and off but did not stay, not even for a forage, and would quickly return to their shelter amongst the deep pack of lifeless mace across the pond.

The island just sat there and just blended into the backdrop, not even a significant feature in itself. It still attracted attention, catching the notice of promenaders, and even comment upon seeing the floating island apparently move, not realising it was just that and only moored in position! That was it, however; sad to say, it was not a particular attraction to the feathered community at all, or so it did appear.

The 'housekeeping' proceeded. The hedging was completed, the dredging accomplished and the banks tidied and manicured. The winter, also, proceeded, as winters do: oft-times, mild and wet; oft-times, cold and chill! Britain has a maritime climate, or as my alma mater geography teacher, good old Mr. Freestone, was ever wont to maintain: "We don't have a climate; we have weather!"

The Christmas and New Year merriment passed with pudding a-plenty under our belt. Spring arrived and the pond sprung readily back to life. The Mallards returned. Then, with much ado and great aplomb, the Canadas arrived, dropped off their pair to resident awhile over the summer, and flocked upon their way.

The Mallards went straightway plunging and dipping, foraging about the bank in a gleeful foray, investigating every nook and hook and cranny but, seemingly, oblivious quite to the new addition to their summer abode! They paddled and waddled but ne'ery a glance was saved it. Only when the Canadas came swooping in did they begin to pay attention to it but, even so, more curious at the Canada's interest than in the island feature itself!

They all paddled urgently in pursuit of the Canadas, around and around this new feature that had now caught their interest, both curious and wary but, also, anxious not to miss out on something! The hoity Canadas seemed quite taken with it, and with the interest they had aroused in the Mallards, and honked and hooted in great delight. Then, feathers flew as, with a great commotion and a flap of wings, they leapt aboard!

The Mallards, of course, were not to be outdone and quickly followed. The floating island bobbed and bounced, lurched, and tugged against its moorings but they held firm. The stipa, now tall and lanky and well-established, shuddered and jolted in some dismay at the unwarranted intrusion as the scurrilous Mallards, thoroughly disrespectful, stomped around encouraging stern and disapproving glances from the Canadas!

Then came calls from across the pond. A sharp 'Kruk!' shrieked out. Another answered in reply. A splash followed. 'Ku-rik!' shrieked back the response, and another in quick succession! The Moorhens tore from their cover, parting the fresh stems of mace that now formed a dense curtain with the hanging strands of withy breaking bud across the far bank. The reeds cracked, yielding only in protest.

Absolutely enthused, the Moorhens continued to cry out to each other, in total disregard, in tones harsh and loud that sliced the chill decorum of the morning air. Sedate and unconcerned, or unperturbed, the stand of willow opposite gave a shrug of nonchalant disinterest!

With a gleeful cacophony, in chorus with the throng that now occupied the floating island - and as if they were being urged on to do so - with a flap of their wings, legs outstretched and trailing behind them, paddling, patting, splashing the water, the Moorhens scooted across the pond to join them aboard. There was much fussing and jostling that followed but the invasion was complete!

Gatwick Park Days - *A Gardening Memoir*

The occupiers fast made good their residence, each in their own little nook staked out and claimed as their own, a community coddled together in mutual support, and so it then proceeded as the days grew longer.

About Eastertide, the familiar, melodic, gargling calls exchanged between the Moorhens arose, that heralded the arrival of their first brood. Within days, the smug and eager quacks and 'quareks' in quick and rapid succession, announced the Mallards own new arrivals! They were all now busy about the pond gaining nibbles, scraps and titbits for their hatchlings.

It wasn't long before the Moorhens were taking their fledgling brood for a short excursion about their island retreat. Occasionally, a loud and abrupt hiss would come from across the fringes of the pond or up on the grassy bank as, feeling threatened, they would see off some predator, real or only perceived as such, and protectively shepherd the Moor-chicks back to safety!

The Mallards, too, were proudly promenading their clutch, the drake riding shotgun, escorting the hen playing follow my leader with her chicks. The ducklings followed her every move. The Mallard is a devoted but quite careless parent, however. In the coming weeks, she would lose not one but two and more of her charges during her transactions abroad and about the precincts of the pond and stream.

In all the years the Canadas paid us service with their visits, never once did they nest but the once the gander was taken by the fox. The provision of our humble floating island, however, had raised an excitement in them to raise their own little brood along with their avian cohabitants aboard and the familiar stack-pile of their nest became clearly visible from afar such that it came to the attention of the Works Manager who remarked upon it with unmistakable concern. The island appeared to have created the perfect invitation for them but a problem for us...

Some days following this intervention, we had further discourse about the turn of events. The idea for the floating island, after all, had come from him and he appeared always to express a favourable interest in its affairs. John elaborated on the apparent uneasiness in his manner.

He kept a motor boat on the Thames, of which he was immensely proud and often made mention of in our many conversations. One year, he was elected Commodore, an honorary title, and he was immensely proud of that, also. He went into a long and detailed explanation, drawing on his knowledgeable observations and personal experience of the creatures.

Gatwick Park Days - *A Gardening Memoir*

The Canadas had populated and overrun whole islands up and down the river and swathes of the bank, also, ruining the habitat entirely, both for themselves and everything and everyone else. He was thinking ahead and of how this might all pan out for our own humble water features should something similar proceed.

Outcomes and consequences are not always things that immediately spring to mind when setting out on a project or course of action, particularly when following what appears to be a spiffing brainwave such as creating something like a floating island and, even John, planner that he was and had to be, as his job demanded, had not considered this one!

A plan was put in place to pull the island to shore and destroy the eggs. There was nothing else for it. The Canadas are a naturalised species, not indigenous to this country, and have swamped other water fowl populations over the years. The introduction of creatures, alien to the habitat, always invites issues, such as the Mink which have escaped into the wild and are diminishing rapidly the humble water vole population.

The escape of Surrey's parakeets, too, that urban legend has it are descended from a pair that were released from Jimi Hendrix's apartment in South London, have flourished in number locally around Reigate's Priory Park. Others believe the rather more mundane theory that they are escapees from the nearby Gatwick Zoo and Aviaries! What effect they have had on native species I cannot say but they must have impacted in some way or manner to deprive them of food or habitat or both.

So, the day came. John undertook to do the deed himself, being familiar with the birds. It is a common method used to legally control goose numbers by preventing their eggs from hatching; this is done by pricking, oiling, or removing and replacing them with dummy eggs. It was the former that had been decided upon.

When their little island started to move, with a jolt and a lurch across the pond, the occupants became quite startled and evacuated with haste! They abandoned ship! Then, alarmed or amazed - I know not which; perhaps, it was both or a modicum of each - they looked on, helplessly, as their home set a course for shore.

Deed done - it took but a moment - and without ceremony, the islet was re-launched and set sail. It was restored, once more, to its former place of rest! The flustering, flamboyant Moorhens, the bombastic Mallards, the blustering, pompous Canadas, their lively trepidation all resolved, took stock, returned, but with some sedate caution, to inspect with great bewilderment the entire startling event that had interrupted their morning agenda! Each climbed, hopped, bobbed back aboard and, seeing nothing, apparently, amiss, resumed their daily routine and went about the chores the day demanded.

The year progressed, the years passed and the floating island settled in to become a permanent feature - and talking point amongst those who took a promenade and observed the island to, apparently, drift with the pull and tug of the wind! No, surely not!

As for the Canadas, they continued to visit but, never more, nested - to John's great relief and satisfaction.

GATWICK PARK DAYS: 5

The Floating Island: Post Script

The floating island settled happily in the midst of the pond, I was at a loose end on where to place the duck house. The solution came to me in a flash: I would turn it into a stilt house in the newly excavated pond. Apart from its practical application, it would present a feature to provide interest and, having secured four sound stakes, the task was undertaken. I would use these as raised piles to make a platform to sit the duck house on and this I proceeded to do.

It had to be sited such that it could be viewed easily from above, on the bank of the stream. It had to look not out of place but to give a pleasant and agreeable aspect. I settled on a spot and retrieved the sledge hammer and waders from the shed. The piles went in quite readily and soundly. There was no room for error in their placement. The suction was such, as they went in, that it would be a gargantuan task to remove and reposition them. Still, it was this that made short but strenuous work of it. All that there was to do now was to knock together a suitable platform.

Gatwick Park Days - *A Gardening Memoir*

A small pallet is already a ready-made platform and I had spied one in the skip just the day before which, with modification, would suit the purpose well. So it was and this was nailed soundly home to the awaiting supports. All that remained was to transport the duck house from its current solitary abode on the bank.

The humble wheelbarrow is a most serviceable and useful and adaptable garden accoutrement, universal in its application. It was only natural to use this to bear the duck house cum stilt house across to the small pond and thence, bizarre as it may sound, into the shallows aside the awaiting platform! With a lug and a heave it was sitting home and sound upon its seat a sight to see.

One additional thing remained to be done, of course, as is most often the case when carrying out plans and taking decisions 'off the cuff' as it were. A means of access for the avian inhabitants had to be provided. There was nothing available that I could appropriate for this purpose for some weeks before a duckboard ramp of sufficient shallow incline could be assembled, put in place and complete the task, but completed it was – finally!

GATWICK PARK DAYS: 6

The White Swan

Of all the avian visitations to grace our much renowned hospital grounds, the most odd and, possibly, the most remarkable, must be that of the White Swan. I say, most odd and most remarkable; perhaps, I should add to this – most brief! It may appear to you that these are most overconfident claims to make but I shall here relate the circumstance of them to you and you may judge for yourself upon the matter.

It was a fine, spring mid-morning. The Willows were a joy to see about the pond, buds breaking new leaf reflecting in the sheen. A span of stems they were, their withies delicate fronds going for a dip, in a splash as it were, as if to test the water! The banks were a lush green of fresh new shoots pushing through last year's stubble of Loosestrife, Astilbe and Aruncus. Life, that had lain dormant through the long winter chill, was once again returning, restored in full bluster, vigorous, vibrant, strong!

The car parks had already filled. The dynamo of human traffic had arrived in full force to spark the hospital motor back into another busy day of

Gatwick Park Days - *A Gardening Memoir*

much to-do. The flood spilled onto the footpath and milled along the drive in a crush of human jetsam. At first, but a trickling stream it was. The stream soon became a great influx as the staff, here employed to administrate, to diagnose and determine care, to nurse and to attend more humble but essential tasks, arrived on the scene.

Then the 'customers' turned up, arriving to attend an early appointment, to visit, or to – whatever else it was their business at that early hour to be here. The trickle had become a flow but soon transformed into a tidal bore against the outflux of night staff departing to end their shift.

Such a busyness it was, of all and sundry quite intent upon their purpose of entering and exiting, and quite perplexing to behold! Then, but the stragglers were left to come and go and a sedate calm attended once again upon the scene.

The hurly of the rush-hour foofaraw and fuss at a standstill, I was left standing now, quite alone, alongside the drive upon the broad open grass stretch kept hand-mown for good appearance. It was but an outcrop of the field, not a lawn by any means, but it looked so much the better for the care and attention it received.

The stripes ever stood out to good effect, but especially so on a day such as this one was, the mowing all freshly done the day before, the grass still damp-dry from an early dew. This hand-mown swathe of turf was ably set off, too, by the line of budding Crataegus along the verge, and to really good effect. It was so effective that it had been drawing the attentive eye of one of the stragglers left sauntering along the footpath and, spying me there, at a loose end so to speak, he seized upon the opportunity to make inquiry. He called me over, with some great enthusiasm, to ask how the stripes could be obtained.

I demurred at his eagerness that, really, it was no special art or skill to achieve this; any mower with a suitable roller might accomplish the same or better. The stripes are only the effect of the blades being rolled forward as the mower proceeds. Thus, the action of simply mowing up and down will have the outcome of the grass blades rolled flat away and flat toward the observer, creating the illusion of a light and dark swathe. It had not been my intention: I was making little of myself but he thought I had been making little of him in asking such a thing. I tried to set matters right but he walked off in a fuss and a hurry and a fluster.

The brief exchange had left me troubled and perturbed that I might have caused such offence but it was done and no recrimination of any sort would set it right but I scolded myself in any case that a better choice of words might have made all the difference. Perhaps, he had hoped for and expected some complicated explanation and it was this that had upset him. Sometimes, a simple answer is insufficient. The intelligent mind ever seeks out the more complex, the more elegant solution and nothing short of that will suffice.

Still, here was adequate provision of solace in the scene I surveyed. All was quite idyllic! Chicks and ducks and geese were all a scurry across the flood plain; a scuttle and a scuffle about their daily chores. It was just perfect, almost too perfect if that is possible, and I paused awhile to view the pleasant vista of the pond's aspect, to soak it up while I might before starting about my own responsibilities. While I might, indeed, for, just then, a squabble of avian voices arose!

A quarrelsome rabble of sparrows hurled itself at the trees behind me and I turned to see the creatures - somehow, but I know not how - just barely avoiding collision with the mat and mesh of branches. The brawl chased uproariously from limb to limb, from tree to tree, all along the line of them that faithfully followed the line of the drive. The pandemonium peaked, then dinned its racket with a clamour off into the distance! As if seizing the shock of silence left behind by their departure, a blackbird chirruped from nowhere in particular at all and warbled a pleasant tune, a pleasure for the hearing juxtaposed with the disharmonious cacophal of the sparrows!

Gatwick Park Days - *A Gardening Memoir*

Down on the flood plain, the Moorhens were purposefully darting, hither and thither, about their business. The Mallards, in full charge about nobody's business in particular, scattered into a dense hide of rush spears. On the far side of the pond, where the fresh reed mace spikes jutted, thrusting through the water, grasses shuddered and jogged merrily in the nuisance and hurry of a mischievous draught of wind scooting by. A large nondescript fish broke water, plopped, plunged, and ripples were sent puddling in ever-increasing arcs and circles across the still and pristine film of the pool. All seemed set - and all the signs were - for another perfect day.

Standing on the grassy ridge above the flood plain, I stood, the observer, as though the lord of my domain. There was barely a breeze at all now. It was as if the world was a stage; the supporting cast had performed their repertoire and the main character, the protagonist of the piece was about to enter the scene. Aloft, the clouds just sat there, a frieze pasted onto the blue canopy in the bright sunlight, big and billowy. A heavy silence fell, only to be disturbed, just the once, by a brief clangor and discordance of impatient Mallards. All was swaddled as it were in a woolly envelope, unreal almost, but a dream and other-worldly. I was enmeshed thoroughly, coddled in my reverie.

Gatwick Park Days - *A Gardening Memoir*

After some few minutes, I became aware of a willowing noise, above me so I thought but from no apparent, placeable or identifiable source. It was as if of a withy swaying and whipping in the tug and pull of the wind. I looked about me and, as much and carefully as I looked, saw nothing I could match the sound with; nothing untoward to see to which I could attribute its source. Yet, there it was, audible and clear, and my wondering was inexhaustible what it could be.

All the comings and goings, briefly, abated, I stood, the lone figure out upon the prow of the grassy ridge. Foolishly, I pictured myself as one of those carved figureheads that sit on the bowsprits of sailing ships of old, chasing through the choppy seas! My Great Uncle sailed in one such ship, a tall-masted clipper, at sea for months on end! On shore leave, his habit was always to descend the stairs backward, as he would at sea! Meandering that memory, absorbed deep in my imaginings, I gazed out across the busy avian thoroughfare of the silent pool. Then... again, the sound! I was stunned awake from my nautical adventuring.

Whatever was it? From wherever did it come? I looked down upon the placid face of the pond and imagined it that choppy sea through which I chased, pursuing some desperate quest, some New World to discover and explore. Then was I

Gatwick Park Days - *A Gardening Memoir*

snatched from my musing by a sight veritable and remarkable to see!

Overhead, a great blur impressed itself upon my view. Shaken so from my imaginings, I thought at first it to be an albatross, or perhaps some such other broad-winged ocean-going bird! So large it was or so did appear but, no, it was not. Still, it was something easily quite as unusual and foreign to our grounds. What was this strange, exotic creature? A white swan!

The creature sailed gracefully, wings slung on the up-draught wind, spread like great, white canvas sheets, fleet, sure, neck shot straight out in front, slim, like a schooner; and I, poor landlubber that I was, stood grounded to the spot! From whence he came I knew not, cared not. The beautiful creature was here, gracing our skies, perhaps to visit awhile and become acquainted – he with us, and us with him – and with our humble grounds.

Overhead he flew, making a crow-line direct toward the beckoning pool glistening enticingly in the sharp-shadowed sunlight. From the steep slope of the grassy ridge where I stood, I looked down and followed him with my keen gaze as he attempted to come in for a landing upon the glassy stretch which spread before him like a table laid. He glided in for a graceful touchdown. Then, at once, appearing to misjudge his descent, he shot off into the blaze of sun!

Gatwick Park Days - *A Gardening Memoir*

I lost him momentarily. Then, there he was once again, circling overhead, as though assessing the situation, or awaiting landing permission from the Gatwick air-traffic control! The control tower must have signalled some assent because, just at that moment, he came in for a second descent.

Head craned forward, sleek, this avian Concorde glided down, across the flood plain, this time, his flight path calculated, apparently, more certainly, more confidently. He came in low, clipped the Salix tips at the pool's edge, leaving the withies swaying back and forth behind him in a wild dance, sprinkling pussies bright and golden like confetti. Wings folded forward in a swift and skilful slowing manoeuvre, he paddled the still surface, leaving ripples startling out, all at once, in all directions around him!

Yet again, he stalled, uncertain, hesitating. He seemed, as it were, strung from wires, at a puppet-masters whim. The great powerhouse of his wings, like topsails, swept; then once, twice, in panic, thumped the still morning air. It appeared he had miscalculated, overshot his planned landing site and this vain second attempt was, likewise, aborted.

His wings flapped urgently to divert some divined disaster, apparent to the pilot but not to any other; not to this awestruck observer, certainly. He rose, almost vertically, glanced across the floating island, surprising the nesting Moorhen who, with lively trepidation, leapt into the water!

The great swan, gleaming white in the arching sun as it approached its zenith, as surprised as was the Moorhen, climbed steeply, neck still craned, head sidewise glancing, seeking his whereabouts. This was an amazing spectacle indeed, and there was I, the only witness, or so I was aware, to its passing.

Up he climbed, up. The great weeping willow at the far side of the pond blocked his path. Miscalculation upon miscalculation! It appeared, briefly, a certitude that there would be such a nasty collision that it would bring him crashing down, crushing his graceful body on the hard surface below. It was the decision of a moment. Taking evasive action, up, up into a steeper climb he soared, this avian pilot. Up, up he coursed, until it seemed he would, indeed, just clear the pinnacle of the great tree.

The long and leafy curtain of withies swayed in a gentle dance before him. He faltered. Perhaps, they were a distraction. No, he would not! Some collision was almost certain. Bird met tree and – somehow, I know not quite how – he clung on there, as if for dear life! Impossible sight so it was to see: this great, white, graceful feathered creature, at home on water and in air, certainly, – but perched some fifteen metres up, precariously

Gatwick Park Days - *A Gardening Memoir*

clinging on, somehow, I know not how, in a great cathedral of a tree? No, surely not!

I - I just stood there and beheld the sight, agog, agape, amazed, speechless. His great white wings spread, keeping his balance like a tightrope walker, a big top performer; he yet maintained his precarious perch! For how much longer he would, I could not summon a guess and still he sat there, yet maintaining his balance, the withies swatting him as his great bulk bent their slender stems, swaying like delicate palm fronds about him. He held on to his purchase with a sheer determination I could only admire him for! He could not, surely, keep his hold for much longer.

The bird there sat for some few minutes more. The withies sagged and swayed uncertainly, the creature, all the while, becoming more and more fearful and agitated by his uncertain situation. He jogged and jerked and jerked and jogged, and held on, as though his wings were very arms, to the flimsy scatter of lithe and supple sprigs and hugging them with all his might. Cling on he did, indeed, and for dear life! Then, at last, finally, the inevitable happened.

The white swan, on water and on wing a great and graceful creature, slipped most ungracefully from his uncertain and precarious perch atop the great cathedral of a tree! Wings flapped, slapped the air furiously. The withies bowed and bent, sending bright, leafy tips showering down. Tree and bird parted company in a most disagreeable manner!

Impossibly, he seemed to hang there in the bright morning air, suspended by some unseen safety wire, this circus acrobat, his performance at a close! He dropped! His wings, like Dumbo's ears, swished and beat the air with violent, massive force; wild, uncertain, they thumped and walloped in fearful confusion but, all the while, maintaining his situation. They smacked the air with such a force and din I thought they must, with all certainty, break. Somehow, his fortitude and composure returned and he regained that self-assurance that creatures of his kind must have to take to the air and soar.

This avian Dumbo believed! In the end, faith is all we have to sustain us. His broad wings spread, expansive, wide, unrestrained by self-doubt. Up and up, he sailed, long neck craned out in front once more, in that Concorde pose he had assumed before, restoring some measure of his confidence and dignity it seemed, but leaving the undercarriage of his feet still dangling, paddling urgently behind, as he disappeared into the distant haze.

I looked about me, lone observer as I was - sole watcher, audience as far I could determine – and felt a sense of privilege to have witnessed such a spectacle. The Big Top had paid us a visit, brief but extravagant and put on a star presentation for my eyes alone. As for the avian residents down upon the flood plain, they expressed no such apparent interest, certainly, in the proceedings. The Moorhen had regained her composure and restored herself to the safety of her island nest, dismissive or unaware of the startling event, or condescending of such indignity and disgrace!

This sight, this performance – not rehearsed, not at all, and yet so perfect in its comic timing, staged, Chaplin-like, completely without cue or cue board - was put on for my edification only as it did seem or so I did suppose. Sole spectator, onlooker, then, it was left to me to regard, record and to appreciate the spectacle. It had been mine and mine alone and, with haste, I jotted the detail down upon the notebook of my eyes to later order into some credible and sensible sequence and make permanent record in the diary of my mind and, thence, make testimony upon these pages.

GATWICK PARK DAYS: 7

The Grand-Daddy Pike

The main water feature was of an indeterminate depth. Some said three metres, some said thirty! Of course, the latter would be too ridiculous to contemplate and the former was the more likely of the two estimations but such statements were considered, at least by myself, to be less in the realm of fact than in that of guesstimation and fantasy. Even so, these grounds were once, so I had been reliably informed by some, the site of abandoned quarry workings.

Perhaps, such extravagant estimations were not so much fantasy, then, nor so far removed from the truth and we, both advocate and sceptic, supporter and detractor, might ably have settled upon a compromise between the two. For some, however, settled upon their own theories and opinions on the matter, there could be no compromise.

Perhaps, a leaf out of the old river boat practice of sounding the depths might not have been amiss and we could have fathomed it for sure and settled the argument once and for all! We had no boat, however, and no paddle to row it with; otherwise we could have taken a "hand lead" - a rope with a heavy weight fastened to its end - and found its mark. The rope is usually twenty-five fathoms long and is marked in increments from twain to twenty fathoms. That would surely have been sufficient to find its mark!

Whichever way it was, truth or fiction, fact or fantasy, our little pond was home to its very own 'Loch Ness Monster' and, somewhere, down in the gloom and dark of that murky depth, there was 'Something' lurking! Just as an astronomer may reliably tell the presence of some distant object, not by an actual sighting of it, but by some determinate effect of its passing upon its environs, so the evidence gradually accrued and mounted to suggest that some 'presence' did, in fact, reside there, down in the dark and murky, indeterminate depths of the pond.

That this could be some supernatural force or some malignant creature of the deep coughed up from the pits of the ocean bottom was, simply, just too bewildering to contemplate and was very quickly dismissed as just too, too fanciful. Still, doesn't everyone, to be absolutely fair, just love a tall tale? So it was that eye-witness observations and 'Chinese whispers' both conspired to build the body of evidence and provide a reputation to create a legend.

Gatwick Park Days - *A Gardening Memoir*

Although it was quite, quite too ridiculous, certainly outrageous to consider such a thing, that our delightful little pond might hide some 'worme' or Ouroboros; conceal some Ogopogo or ancient Plesiosaur, or merely some other little known, more mundane but terrible creature, some still cradled the idea and gave it credulous consideration. Those few verily loved a tall tale to engage others in and what better than a home-spun yarn to enlarge upon and elaborate, particularly to newcomers and visitors? Readily pencilled on their quick tongues was this fable, to repeat and to tell to any and everyone, visitor or passer-by, they might encounter - or collar and waylay - willing to stop the while and lend an ear and listen and allow themselves to be so cajoled and persuaded.

And so they did, and so did the evidence continue to accrue with which to argue their case. After dark, upon bright and moonlit nights, there were infrequent but constant reports of loud plops and of an eerie shape breaking the water across the glossed and silvery slick of the smooth and pondering glassy surface. Such nocturnal observers, their wild speculations spurred on and spurring them on by such stretches of the imagination that had been circulating and, also, an eager willingness to lend them credibility, allowed themselves to perceive all manner of shadows and darting ripples and wakes as a veritable family of these unidentified swimming creatures – 'USC's as they became known to that dedicated band, the rare and exclusive circle of the Strange Phenomena Club!

All-night vigils were set up to log whatever might occur. Accurate record keeping was a paramount concern of the Strange Phenomena Club (Povey Cross Section). The 'Povey Cross Section' was, actually, the only section of the club existent. Still, the appendage looked good, sounded good and lent their little club of just three members more dignity, more credence and credibility to the outsider if it appeared that these steadfast few were just part of a wider network of such 'investigators' and, perhaps, made them appear less foolish, less of a tiny 'lunatic fringe' than otherwise it would have done!

The subjects of their investigations were particular and several. There were the strange disappearances of the duck-chicks, for example. Was it all down to the dozy carelessness of the laidback Mallards, or was there something more sinister at work? What, after all, of the culling of the Moor-chick batch? Could that be so readily explained away? Such a thing could not be said of the Moorhens; these were ever so meticulous and watchful parents in their doting care, rallying their offspring to their side at every twist and turn. No, there had to be more to this, surely. There had to be some solution to these events more sinister than what might appear at first sight.

So diligent, so conscientious were these delightful creatures, lavishing such dutiful and abounding attention upon their young and upon each other, that it would really be quite unfair and unkind to assume such a thing of them, that they were of a likewise careless nature as were the Mallards. Then, what was it at work here? What, indeed? There was a surplus of questions and a surfeit of explanations. It did indeed appear to be the case, however, that there was just the one and only one conclusion to arrive at. What else but that there was, almost certainly, something rather more menacing and nasty at work, lurking there in the deep?

Yes, this phenomenon was a top notch matter for investigation all right. It was right up there with crop circles, of which there was at least one notable manifestation less than eight kilometres distant! It was certainly on a par with the weird faerie lights that infrequently appeared on damp, chill nights, seen darting hither, thither and playing at the pond's fringes. It was certainly of more deserving attention, surely, than the faerie rings at the top of the drive!

Now, these faerie rings deserve some comment or mention in themselves and here might be an appropriate occasion to do just that! There was an elderly lady who lived just along the road from our hospital. She was a dear old soul. Upon enquiring of her name, I was informed by some sage colleagues that this was Dotty. Whether or not that was actually her name or it was a description of her mental state, I will have to leave to others more qualified to determine. However, I shall always think of her as Dotty, not 'dotty'!

Dotty would regularly pass by upon her perambulations, oft-times being led by a little pooch of dubious parentage. This little chap would dart this way and that, ever hunting out the next interesting scent to scrutinise. He would always stop off for a good sniff around our patch of grass bordering the footpath and have a course through the hawthorn hedge, just like a 'regular' dropping in at the local watering hole! There were messages to leave and messages to read, left by others of his kindred who had passed that way. This is how those of his kind communicate with each other, after all, and this was, if you will, a veritable post box and sorting office for them.

Of course, Dotty would have to stop off as well; she had not much choice in the matter, after all. Then, what better recourse than to do likewise and to take the opportunity to have a chat and friendly gossip upon the events of the day with whomsoever of her kindred should there happen to be present upon their perambulations up and down the drive? And should I, by happenchance, be there present as, infrequently, I would be, either mowing, hedging, or about whatever business I was about, then who more convenient to chat with than this dear lady? And that was how we first became acquainted.

The conversation would start the way of most all conversations: we would talk about the weather! Other topics of the day would then soon ease their inevitable way in, following the scent so to speak of the one previous, by logical sequence or progression. Others, stumbled into like a puddle, would splash up and take our attention, seizing us serendipity-like, scooting off onto entirely different directions – in a fashion, not so very unlike Dotty's little pooch, charging into thickets of laurel, as he would, and then snuffling round the stand of silver birch! Perhaps, after all, we do share some crossover gene; I think that may be the case, I really do. Pooch, people, we aren't so very different in our social habits.

So it came about that I learned of the wee folk who inhabited our grounds. Dotty assured me – by way of casual information or to lend weight to the veracity and verisimilitude of her tale, I know not which – that the famous and renowned author, H G Wells himself, no less, had written in sincere belief upon the subject of the certain existence of the faerie folk and was fully prepared to give just consideration to whatever evidence might be presented by those who would further the case for such a submission. Why, the very authority of the reputation of the man spoke for itself, she said!

I said nothing untoward in return, of course, nor could I; indeed, the very thought did not even enter my mind to do so for such a thing would have been a disrespectful and unkind thing to do. I passed neither comment nor aside and made neither remark nor digression but, in their stead, expressed a non-committal and polite interest. I could not do otherwise, unwilling to shatter such a sincerely held belief and cause offence to the dear lady. Still, nonetheless, I will admit I was curious; I am open to stretching the bounds of common belief if the evidence will support the premise. Succinctly, I was prepared to hear her out and give the story fair scrutiny.

Apparently, Dotty had had recourse to visit late the superstore residing adjacent to our site. It backed on at the rear, but there was no through access via our property. It therefore entailed a long and tiresome traipse for her to follow the road all the way round. However, her need had demanded the effort and dragged her out. The dark autumn evenings were closing in and, as she passed by upon her return journey, Dotty caught sight of movement upon the long, grassy strip that runs the full length of the drive, toward its approach to the road. Her interest and curiosity thus aroused, her shopping clutched tightly and neatly in the one hand, she peered beneath the peak cap of the other, thus permitting her eyes, still keen and alert, to become accustomed and adjust to the awkward play of light.

The parade of lamps gleamed and glanced; the last rays of evening collapsed into a heap beneath the rooftops. Yes, she was certain. There were, indeed, shadows playing upon the newly mown sward. Dotty ventured down the footpath into the grounds, - with great caution, as she said, so that she should not give fright to what creature it might be – either natural, or supernatural – that frolicked there. Then, as she did relate to me, Dotty paused; she looked and had to look twice more! A look of genuine wonderment dawned and a sincere bewilderment stretched clean across her shocked countenance. "Imagine, my dear," she insisted, overwhelmed absolutely by her utter enthusiasm, "my complete surprise to find not some natural fauna but some faerie folk dancing in such a gay abandonment there!"

Now, those are her very words in their entirety and I have reproduced them faithfully here that any may make of them exactly what they will. I asked what she did then and what did they upon seeing her. Did they not take offence that she had witnessed their nocturnal goings on and activities? Nor did they not make sore grievance with her? Well they might have as, by repute and by tradition, fae folk do readily take slight and great exception at the most innocent and blameless of intrusions into their affairs! She replied that they did not, or did not appear to do so. Moreover, they betrayed not any sense of awareness of her presence at all. "It was all so unreal and otherworldly," the dear lady assured me.

So, there they were those faerie folk, all leaping most gaily, by her report, flitting in and out the shadows, oblivious to all but their very own endeavours. And what did Dotty then? She left the oat cakes which were her purchase at the superstore upon the grass there for their pleasure. Her eyes grew clouded; her appearance donned an expression of great caution and concern and, in all seriousness, she informed me, in a most solemn and sincere tone: "To keep their hurt and harm at bay!" Dotty was nodding her head most vigorously now and, with a genuine gravity of voice, further insisted: "For you have to make your peace with the fae folk, else they will, most assuredly, give vent to their mischief and play some dreadful prank or monkey business on you!"

The following morning, so she said, the oat cakes had all gone absent from the lawn and her little pooch did not dare to venture onto the hospital grounds. For all her coaxing, this state of affairs persisted for more than a week before the little chap would again venture in to pick up his mail! Make of it what you will, that is the tale and there it stands. I have related the encounter truthfully and that is sufficient. It is what it is.

As I have brought you to this juncture, it may be of interest to mention that there here resided, in a property adjoining ours and quite adjacent to the drive, a certain neighbour who was ever available for the opportunity of a chat, or a grumble - should I be there also present and available - about the condition of the boundary wall which separated her property from the hospital grounds. Now, I may be digressing, and more than slightly, from the main thread of my story but I do crave your indulgence; should that be the general consensus of opinion prevailing, I do further beg your forbearance, but this dear lady is deserving of some mention somewhere for she did, indeed, have the right to be somewhat 'miffed' so to speak.

This wall of hers ran the length of the drive into the main body of the property. It hid behind the Hawthorn hedge and divided, as I have already related, her property from ours. There were cracks forming in various and diverse places due to settlement or subsidence and also, I might add, due to the encroachment of the dreaded Japanese Knotweed which I did my utmost to discourage and keep under control. This I did to some good effect simply by knocking down the fresh spring shoots and by not permitting any further growth to mature. This practice did have some great measure of success in restraining its spread and keeping it in check. It was a simple enough task to run the hoe along as I proceeded with the hedge trimmer, decapitating the crowns.

There had been a history of problems. A ten metre section of the wall had actually been summarily demolished some years previously during major ongoing building works. This mishap of catastrophic dimensions to the dear lady occurred during the implementation of the projected second phase construction of two supplemental wings at the rear of the hospital and other many and diverse associated works that wreaked quite some disruption and extensive havoc at times to our daily working lives, not to mention the discomfort and nuisance inflicted on 'The Passengers' as my associate was wont to call our customers, or 'patients' as they are referred to in the public sector!

How this calamity occurred was this way: A contractor was manoeuvring his oversized and cumbersome vehicle along the narrow approach drive. Descending at an overconfident pace, the disastrous collision resulted! Of course, the responsibility for making good and restoring the wall fell to us. This was not merely because it was the builder's contractor who had caused this terrible damage and was, therefore, our responsibility; that is not what most miffed this now distraught dear lady. No, this was another matter entirely, and of long standing.

The tale, as I heard it second hand, is thus: that, while the initial groundwork for the hospital construction was being undertaken, a projected through access route at the rear of the site, which has now been given over to a housing development and recreation area on Withy Meadows, for reasons that I am unclear about, became unavailable for that purpose. Therefore, an adequate and suitable access to substitute for this loss was of paramount importance. This became, thenceforward, the prime consideration of the project.

A bungalow, "Brookdale", had been purchased, at great cost, to provide an entry point by employment of the side portion of its grounds. However, this planned use of the garden was hardly sufficient to provide both a point of entry and egress. When this dear lady of whom I speak learned that the construction work in progress adjacent to and at the rear of her property was for the purpose of providing a hospital – an admirable amenity, surely! – she permitted her altruistic good sense to gain the better of her rational judgement and to find a ready place in her charitable heart. She took it upon herself to resolve the issue for them!

Gatwick Park Days - *A Gardening Memoir*

Having learned of the dilemma that now confronted the developers, she readily donated, gratis, the side section of her garden for the very purpose of providing such adequate access and egress! An undertaking was made, by way of acknowledgement and in recognition of her profound generosity, to construct and maintain an adequate dividing wall the full length of her extensive garden. As evidenced by the cracks, this we have pitifully neglected to do and have woefully failed her in – at least, adequately – and circumstance, certainly, contrived, it would seem, to confirm that view.

The topic would invariably and inevitably, raise its tedious head. Whether due to encroachment of the Knotweed or else to an inattentive and negligent attitude to maintenance, the cracks, in plain sight on her side but, on ours, concealed conveniently behind the Hawthorn, would ever spring up to intrude in our exchanges. They were an eyesore for her. Curiously, however, there was not a sign of the weed on her side, or none that I ever perceived.

The Knotweed is a most invasive, non-native plant that surveyors are required to report if they encounter it. The landowner is also required to contain its spread, hence many a lawsuit resulting from spread from railway embankments where, undetected, it has proliferated and, like another non-native species, the Buddleia, made a home and earned a notoriety for itself. Yet, this reviled and dreaded Knotweed is also a notable source of resveratrol providing powerful and potent benefits to health! That is an irony, indeed.

I would ever sympathise, and genuinely so, for whatever representations I might make on her behalf, they would ever fall on deaf ears. Whatever was the sentiment of her own exasperations, those the dear lady would make upon her own behalf would meet with a similar reception, or so it would appear, to gain a favourable response to her petitions. I once pleaded with her, without thinking – so does irony mock us – that it was like banging your head up against a brick wall. To which the good lady quite merrily quipped: "...About a wall!" In the end, at last, it was only to have a moan, then. It appeared so. It does us all good, sometimes, to have a moan, perhaps.

The Strange Phenomena Club (Povey Cross Section) would meet informally – and regularly – over a coffee and toast in the staff restaurant, whenever their shifts coincided to enable this to take place. Note, I do say Staff Restaurant and not staff canteen: this was, after all, a PRIVATE hospital! The talk would ramble about the goings on in their workaday life but ever return to and centre on the USC's that were always a particular and topical subject matter for conversation. Speculation would range from the mundane to the marvellous; from the elegant to the extravagant; from the simple to the simply startling and sagacious.

One of these fine fellow-me-lads was an old sage of some years to his toll, quite past the finishing line of retirement, but still spry and perky. His wit was impeccable. A raconteur of the first order he was and could ever be relied upon to stretch a tall tale further than most, certainly, as far if not further than anyone I have ever met. With no hesitation of forethought, his quick mind would make meat out of the stuffing and construct substance out of the fog of obfuscation. His favourite phrase or saying, his 'call sign' so to speak: "Every day's a bonus!" And the familiar greeting, "How're you?" would ever elicit that expected response: "Every day's a bonus! Every day's a bonus!"

Old Bill was very much the mentor and guide of the group of three. Sometimes, or so it seemed to me, he was only leading the other two on, almost as if just to see how far he could stretch their bounds of belief. At other times, he was so convincing and sincere in his rhetoric that I could scarce but not believe otherwise than accept that he, too, was a true believer. Mentor he may have been but, however dazzling with his seemingly bottomless pit of knowledge of the esoteric and supernatural, this club of theirs was very much a troika of equals.

Gatwick Park Days - *A Gardening Memoir*

Then, one day, there was found floating in the shallows, just beneath the crowd of jostling pussy willows at the water's edge, in amongst the suckers, tangled in the heavy bloom of blanket weed, a great Pike at least a metre in length, the likelihood more, but not a centimetre less! The Pike was slit from stem to stern, not neat as with a fishwife's knife, but serrated and ragged; torn, ripped as by some sharp-fanged beast! No, this was no human hand that caught the fellow and, careless, casually threw him back in. Why, with the very size of him, he would have been a fine trophy for the angler who caught him! It was then, too, that I became convinced this was no Nessie we were dealing with, that haunted those deeps, but – a Grand-daddy Pike!

At the bottom of many a deep and dark, still pool there lurks a Pike and it looked to be that way for ours. The deceased fish was of such a size I began to wonder at and marvel, however, just how large might be the Pike that caught him; how dark and deep a pool might have to be to produce a Pike of such extraordinary size. As for that and as for his extraordinary size, well the hospital grounds were once, many long years gone by, as I have related, the site of an old quarry working. That alone may account for his size, I suppose, and might even supply some means of determination to establish the actual depth of the pool. Still, there was no real telling but only suggestion, for this was a measure and not a rule and no means of any substance to establish just how deep, except to say that very deep it must surely be and deeper far than in anyone's estimation!

This humble interpretation of the facts thus far presented by evidence and observation but stumbled upon failure to persuade the true believers otherwise. The scales were tipped, it seemed, into a dogged insistence that this was only further proof, if further proof were needed! My attempts to demystify the situation failed miserably. Those who do not want to be persuaded will not be convinced. Despite all my protestations to the contrary, still, those old diehards dug in their heels and steadfastly refused to accept the evidence – of logic and what is self-evident as much by simple and straightforward evaluation of the observed events – and continued to dispute simple deduction and assertion.

These few noteworthies, I need not tell for that realisation must be plain enough for any to themselves deduce, were that august and close-knit assemblage of the exclusive and seclusive Strange Phenomena Club (Povey Cross Section). I had attempted to educate them to the fact that some old Grand-daddy Pikes grow large enough and are powerful enough to drag down not merely ducklings and Moor-chicks but babes and even small children. Reports concur such victims have fallen prey to the predatory instincts of their kind.

Indeed, no; no responsible parent should permit their youngster to stray alone abroad a still and silent pool, for it may hold a menace more real and more lethal than any 'worme' or Ouroboros, Plesiosaur or Ogopogo. Down there concealed, far beneath the smooth and placid surface, in some dark and deep recess of the pool, there may lurk something far more tangible and deadly just waiting for what opportunity may present: some old and grumpy Grand-daddy Pike!

GATWICK PARK DAYS: 8

The Grand-Daddy Pike: Post Script

This is just a by the by in regard to the elderly lady who lived just along the road from our hospital: that dear old soul whose name I was informed most reliably by some sage colleagues was Dotty. Whether or not it was their actual belief that this was her name or was simply an expression of poor wit, an unkind opinion as to her mental state, I cannot say. However, I have since discovered her real name and, I may add, that of her little pooch!

It happened this way,- that I was passing by upon my way to work, past the neighbouring properties in Povey Cross Road, a disproportionate number of which, our being in such close proximity to the airport, were guest houses. There were, forever, comings and goings and toings and froings, it seemed, by the dozen. The back and forth, to and from the airport, was almost incessant, for an early flight, late departure or arrival, and so it was that morning.

The proprietor of one of these many lodging places was oft seen loitering about to bid farewell or meet and greet - and, likewise, just so, any passer by who, just by happenchance, was passing by at the time. It had been a nondescript summer, quite unremarkable and, when I fell into an exchange with a fleeting comment upon the current inclement conditions and the peculiarities of our unreliable British weather, the fellow would not let the conversation go and drew me into a lively discussion about the state of the world.

Across the road, the firemen's picket stood sentry outside the fire station about a blazing brazier to keep them warm. This caught his gaze and attracted the immediate, inevitable quip that the firemen were now resorting to starting fires it seemed, like Fahrenheit 451. I acknowledged the comment with a perfunctory grin and he jumped straightway into his usual complaint or comment or two about his neighbour's high laurel hedge. It slipped its predictable way into the conversation quite naturally along with his sage remark that you can choose your friends but you can't choose your neighbours!

For my part, I recalled an incident that had befallen me just that morning upon my pushbike; the very pushbike I had dismounted from to cross the roundabout and was then walking with when I had been accosted by him. A squirrel had appeared from nowhere and shot out barely beneath my front wheel. Moments saved him - and me - from the near collision. The chap

Gatwick Park Days - *A Gardening Memoir*

would have brought me down as well as damaging himself. Then, having made a right turn, challenging the realms of all possibility, the incident was repeated!

Another squirrel darted straight in front, barely missing my wheel, in such a haste across the road, and struck the wheel of the transit passing just at that moment on the other side! The poor creature rebounded off the side wall of the tyre, gathered what wits it had left and continued straightway on its journey into the welcoming shelter of the bushes bordering the road. A moment sooner and he would have been under the wheel, just another statistic for the road to record!

This enjoined him to mention the red gene was returning. Had I not noticed, too, he asked, the predominance of the red bristles appearing amongst the grey? I had to agree that we don't seem to see the true-bred Gray we used to see as kids. I had to confirm his obtuse contention and recounted that those populating Brockwell Park in Brixton in my childhood were all, indeed, a silver gray without a trace of any red-brown bristles and no bushy tail at all to compare with the Red. When the Red returns, he contended, in most solemn tone, we shall have our country back.

The conversation convoluted amiably thus. Then

did the dear lady in question chance into the banter of words between us – myself and this fellow traveller upon the journey of his day. A hurry had engulfed me to return upon mine, else I should surely arrive late but, at this, I permitted the conversation to proceed. Did I know her, he asked, and had I heard? She had come into some money, an inheritance by her account, and would be taking up residence in the property that was part of the bequest. She had insisted, he said, it had come about because of the cautious respect she had shown to the faeries! You mean Dotty, I asserted; no, I was confidently informed, her name was Dorrie, not Dotty, and that of her pooch being, apparently, Lynne!

Now, how about that? However, I will always think of her as I knew her, I think, but affectionately and endearingly so, as Dotty, not Dorrie, and most certainly not - 'dotty'!

GATWICK PARK DAYS: 9

The Garden Fox

Curiouser, and curiouser! Whether it be mere coincidence, synchronicity, or you may call it what you will, but I am confounded. It is not long since that I completed my account of the life and times of Monsieur le Fox of Gatwick Park and entered it all here upon these pages as best and accurately as memory may recall. Not long since, indeed, and thought the matter laid to rest - as old Reynard himself had been laid to rest - when, only this morning in fact, having ventured as far as the bottom reaches of my mother's garden, I was brought to a sudden and jarring halt!

The garden has been left very much to its own devices for many years. My brother has desired a wild garden, an admirable enough goal in the right place and in the right setting. Here, everything is competing for enough room and enough light in what is, after all, a finite space and the garden has become merely an unkempt and untidy disarray. The Leylandii have attained a dangerous height and overhang several other properties besides. The gales of previous winters, and as lately as last winter, have brought down boughs and branches which I have had to attend to at my brother's request. Circumstance imposes its own demands and some new plan of action is necessary.

Therefore, I had been embarked upon a mission of assessment of exactly what measures it might be necessary to adopt to restore all once more to a reasonable and safe condition of general tidiness. Busying myself, jotting down pertinent observations and notes upon scraps of vacant thought, I quietly filed my plans away for future reference. Then, something had drawn my gaze, inexorably, unswervingly, toward the dim-lit shadows beneath the crowded stand of trees.

The morn was yet young but, there, by the wire-mesh fence, and plain as day to see, my eyes perceived a sable form lying prostrate upon a soft bed of pine droppings. It was the garden fox. The garden fox lay there dead. Dead!

Never had I seen him in life but oft had I been alerted to his presence. My brother had remarked upon him on numerous occasions. He had observed the fellow about on his nightly rounds; shot a torch beam through the black gloom and freeze-framed him still as death against the backdrop of the night; caught his eyes, gleaming back at him in the darkness, staring him down! And, now, my turn had come at last and, here, that his sleek form may grace my eyes, he lay – dead.

Gatwick Park Days - *A Gardening Memoir*

There was no emaciation; he had not starved, certainly. He was of a good age, for my brother had spied him out on his nightly jaunts through the rear garden for some two years or more at least. He lay there with such a calm turn to his expression. It was almost a smile that he wore. I can only imagine he had lived his life and his time had come; that it was old age that had taken him. Now, here he lay and if I did not soon lay him to rest then putrefaction would, very quickly if not sooner, claim his corpse and walk off with him. Most certainly; and leave its sweet and sickening stench to haunt the air and tread this woody grove without remorse, without respect.

I scratched away the drab and dusty layering of pine needles with the spade, using it as a rake, made a heap of them and rammed the blade into the fine, compact soil at the base of the tree. The work brought tears of sweat to my brow and tears of melancholy to my eyes as I made a trench sufficient for his size, roughly according to his proportions. It was a snug fit when it came to it. I arranged his rigid body with the tip of the spade, tipped him over carefully in the newly excavated hole, properly observing the deference due to the dead, and cushioned him within its bowels, up against the broad trunk, gnarled and knotted as it was in uniform fashion like a Pirelli tyre.

Coincidences do wear rather thin, I know, and do so commonly occur that it is every wonder that they should cause us to comment upon them at all. Yet, they do continue to rear their heads and to repeat themselves, like some veritable pest or nuisance, to demand our attention, to so perplex and intrigue and, thus, do continue to confound us. Is it the universe, perhaps, drawing us to the attention of our Maker, to humble us to some awareness of Him in our daily life?

Eerier and eerier, for these events, one following in the shadow of the other and strangely linked by circumstance – 'coincidence' – set off in me a feeling of déjà vu; another common nonsense, I realise, but one more circumstance to add here to bear the burden of 'proof' of the supposition!

All circumstantial? Oh yes, I know this to be true; but 'déjà vu'? Oh, yes, I had been here before, in a familiar setting of circumstance, that is, and I must ask my reader to contain that cry of protest as I am compelled to here relate this. Therefore, do I crave your patience and beg your indulgence – just one more time.

The circumstances of my recollection relate to events of some thirty years previous. At that time, I was working in the British Gas showrooms in Redhill. It was pleasant and steady enough work that kept the all-important pennies coming in. It was a pleasant and steady enough company of fellows in whose company I passed my working day; too pleasant, too steady to have to make such weighty decisions, some might have thought, that were then thrust upon us by the startling circumstances that then arose.

We were little more than an hour into our morning routine when I was approached discreetly – furtively! – by my co-worker, Roy, as most likeable and decent a sort as you could hope to meet. He spoke to me in such hushed whispers that I was compelled to incline my head toward his. His manner and tone were almost conspiratorial. It might have been construed by someone who did not know better that we were up to no good; else we were upon some special mission of subversion involving matters of state and the secret service!

He had made a discovery of some import in amongst the nooks and crannies about the place; one that I had certainly overlooked, even though it surely fell amongst my various duties that I should have chanced upon the discovery myself. To clean and tidy such coves and corners was my remit, after all; and this despite, I should hasten to point out, my arrival upon the premises some half an hour or more before anyone else, providing ample opportunity to do so. So, what was this discovery? It had come to his notice and become a concern that an intruder had forced an entry during the night!

I listened, intent, glued to every word, for I do so

confess that I was aware of nothing contrary that could be amiss. The intruder, so I learned, was of that ill breed of rough-kempt and unbathed individual, long-haired, who had, very probably, not done an honest day's work in all his brief existence. Yet, Roy was concerned for the fellow! This was because intruders of this ilk did not suffer such light a sentence as arrest and imprisonment for their misdemeanour; rather: apprehension, capture and – death! Death...? Yes, death, for this was no ordinary intruder you see, the likes of whom the local constabulary might have expressed an interest in; no, this fellow was of a totally different sort.

Now, Roy was not at all a chap of the kind to stomach such a fate for anyone, particularly for what was, after all, such a seemingly innocuous offence to warrant such a drastic penalty; least of all, for the little chap who we now confronted and who stared back up at us from beneath the racking in the parts store at the rear of the showroom. So, there we stood - the men from UNCLE - two conniving and uncompromising special agents, intent upon contriving some means of providing this interloper with an exit strategy with which to extricate himself from the dire, dire situation - of which he was blissfully unaware - that would surely entrap him should the rat-catcher be summoned!

Gatwick Park Days - *A Gardening Memoir*

Yes, there we stood - I playing a glacial rendition of Illya Kuryakin to his charming presentation of Napoleon Solo, while it was briefly explained to me that he had initially stumbled upon the diminutive intruder while attending to an erring Robinson-Willey. There, snug by the warming glow bulbs that burned within, beneath the imitation, fibre glass coals, he lurked - the rat! And such a sorry rat, of lank and greasy main, that looked up, so sad and apologetic for itself, with twitching whiskers and wan, dewdrop eyes! Small wonder, then, that it had won his heart.

He urged me, pleaded with me, to say nothing of the creature's presence. I needed neither urging nor asking; whatever the bad press and poor reputation attributed to his kind, now being confronted with the wretched little fellow, how ever could I contemplate and devise his demise? And so we said nothing; but: how to keep him a secret from the intrusions and meddlings of the storeman? Now, that presented a problem.

As it turned out, it presented no problem at all. We had determined that I would return with some suitable apparatus to catch the intruder with and attempt to remove him from the building. When I did so later, however, he had already departed from his hidey-hole; there was not a sign of him anywhere. I searched high and low, but it was as though he had never been there at all. The storeman had arrived but made no comment or reference at all as he, most certainly, would have done had he been confronted with a rat, and the day proceeded upon its inevitable, uneventful course and no further mention was made of our little visitor and what may have been his fate.

That evening, back home, I was happily and readily contemplating sitting down with my meal to watch the new John Cleese sitcom. My dad had put me on to it; it concerned a Guest House in Torquay and all the odd goings on there. It had acquired quite a following. That particular evening's presentation concerned a pet which Manuel had come by. The pet turned out to be – a rat! Surely not... Coincidence! Ah yes, 'déjà vu' and synchronicity besides! My eyes gawked; my mouth gaped in astonishment. I could not, did not believe it. Yet, how could I discount and disqualify the evidence of my own eyes before me? Truth is, indeed, stranger than fiction and the comedy of life more comic, more tempered with irony, than any sketch ever devised to be comedic or laced with satire.

Gatwick Park Days - *A Gardening Memoir*

GATWICK PARK DAYS: 10

The Garden Fox Cub

Extraordinary news! Tabby rushed up in a great and terrible commotion and tore through the backdoor; then, confident he had caught my attention, went straightway back into the back garden from whence he had just appeared. He leapt onto the barbeque, all poised and proud, eyes fixed toward the shadows in amongst the tall Leylandii at the bottom. Apologies! Introductions are necessary... Tabby is my mother's feline confidante and companion!

I went to the door to observe what could be up and, there, upon the grass, stood the cub, already showing the self-assured signs of adulthood. He was upright, taut. A cursory gaze from him assessed what threat, what danger we might pose. He was not at all rushed and I turned in a haste to fetch my camera to record the event!

I returned to find him already retreating back into the dim light of the Leylandii's deep shadow. He paused to look back at me. Tabby still watched, unmoved, unmoving. His keen eye could see and pick him out better than my own. I snapped a hasty photo. Too late! The image of him is a blur in the midst of the dark shadows. No matter, I shall keep a watchful eye out and, with Tabby's assistance, endeavour to capture him and, if successful, record his image upon these pages.

I had been hoping for some glad news to report; instead, I have only sad news of dire and tragic consequence! I commenced this diary or log, or call it what you will, to jot down my Gatwick Park days in response to an upheaval that occurred in my life that called me to up sticks, such was the import of circumstance that presented.

My brother had suffered a haemorrhage to the frontal cerebrum. An ambulance was called but was not sent; a paramedic was dispatched in its place. This, perhaps, was not amiss as such as we were not aware, ourselves, of the circumstance of his distress. Yet, neither was the responder come to his aid and who eventually summoned the cavalry to convey him off to hospital. The grim circumstance I am now called upon to record is that he will not recover but has been settled into a nursing home where, now, he resides.

Some twenty years ago, my brother and I topped these very Leylandii that stand so tall and, now, dwarf the silver birch that climbs itself to some 20 metres in height. They stood at a mere 20 metres themselves at that time and we reduced them to ten, I armed with but a bow saw, he with a rope to bring down the boughs as I took them off and my mother to make a bonfire of them.

Leylandii are notoriously fast growing and attain extraordinary heights, becoming the subject of such antipathy and antagonism, even litigation, between neighbours. It is hardly the tree for a smallish garden, you might think, unless kept trimmed and compact, and yet it was the tree of choice for so many for a period not long since ago.

In these twenty years since, growing at a rate of anything up to a metre or more a year, they stand way in excess of 30 metres. I could not reduce these giants, these eight Leylandii of such a height and proportion, even with my brother's assistance, and certainly not without it. The sheer quantity of timber to dispose of would be quite an insurmountable quandary in itself. The prospect was absolutely untenable. Hence, I had resort, on my brother's behalf, to call in assistance in the form of professional help.

The fellows arrived on the set day and took out a fence panel by the line of trees to undertake the task of removal. As this work was in progress, the charge hand drew my attention to a portion of animal carcase lying amongst the debris and detritus of the trees. "What's that," he said, not by way of question but by way of comment. I, seeing the distinctive brush, remarked, "It's a fox!" He, by reply: "A fox cub; I thought it was a cat."

I knew at once it must be our garden fox cub. Whatever could have brought him to this demise? How was this possible? Had another male encountered him and challenged him for his territory? Had he perished on his own without benefit of parental protection and been picked over for his meat by some predator or carrion? I do not know. I removed him to one side while the work proceeded and, later, laid him to rest.

Strange: as convinced as you may be upon the fact of a matter, circumstance will ever prevail to make you question it. What I knew, perhaps, I did not know, at least, with any certainty. It was but a week since the fellow was interred in his final resting place when my certain estimation of the way of the matter was openly challenged by the appearance of clear evidence to the contrary.

Blackie, the other half of the intrepid pair of feline notables who share my mother's house with her, was in yowl mode in the back garden. It was not so much a distress call as that of a lieutenant summoning his troops. It could be clearly heard, as though it were in the room. I went to the door; looked out. Blackie, bold fellow-me-lad that he is, was edging ponderously towards the crab tree, still stooping from the blast of the Great Storm of so long ago. It seemed as though he were stalking something. I played the outrider to his ramrod and, together, we sought out the wayward brush-popper ensconced in his hidey-hole.

A young fox! I surprised him through the shrubbery and he darted off toward the bottom shed and disappeared. Blackie, forearmed and assured by my presence, chased off in pursuit but to no avail. He was gone, like a will o' the wisp, there and not there, a thing of our fancy. Is this my fox cub and was that other, unfortunate that he was, the remains of some interloper? I cannot say. I cannot at all be certain which way it is...

Some days passed and Tabby brought me to the door by his insistence and I followed him outside. There he was again, the fellow, but which he was I do not know! He stood there, calm as day, standing over something – a morsel scavenged from some bin, perhaps. I rushed back in for my camera and snapped him. He was looking straight back at me, nonchalant and quite unperturbed by our presence! Such is the stalwart and certain confidence of the town fox, quite unlike the demeanour and bearing of his country cousin.

Remarkable, quite remarkable is coincidence; a thing of conjecture, its significance insinuates an order in the daily transaction of life, so chaotic, so random in its harsh and conflicting dealings with us, that there may be, after all is said and done, a maker of all, a God Almighty intervening in our lives to guide us if but we would only take heed of that gentle nudge, that quiet prod and listen.

GATWICK PARK DAYS: 11

Another Rats Tale!

John had offered me some timber racking from the workshop. It was no longer required and he thought I might make some good use of it, which, indeed, I had and expressed my genuine thanks to him for it. With just a few suitable and appropriate modifications, it now stood the full length of the shed alongside the windows and served to house the summer bedding, to bring them on and, where appropriate, as with the geraniums, to over-winter. It was a veritable potting shed, which I happily compared with my father's a life-time away.

I was tending to this bedding when I was called most urgently to the door. A silhouette of a figure stood there, stock-still. I recognised her as one of the secretaries from reception. She waited there, uncertain, undecided, and most agitated. It was most concerning to see her so. Adopting a conciliatory demean, I approached her with some measure of caution.

"We've got rats!" The words tumbled out in a rush, short, terse and sharp. It seemed a relief for her to have said it. She relaxed immediately, as

though the words had been boiling up inside her and she was so grateful to have let off steam.

"Rats?" I asked. "Not voles?" Her response was quick and adamant that what she had seen was most certainly a rat. There was no doubt of it. She had been perambulating on a stroll after her luncheon, before her return to duty, when she saw the creature scurry up the bank and into the shrubbery. I knew where she meant at once. It was the bed of dogwood we had planted by the gate, where the stream hooks round the west wing. I took her at her word and assured her I would investigate.

Water voles also live alongside rivers, streams and all manner of freshwater habitats. They are frequently mistaken for rats, in the same manner as Moorhens are mistaken for Coots. They are both distinguished with ease by just one feature of their anatomy, of course: Coots by their lobed feet and the rat by his scaly tail. With that in mind, I determined to find out which or what the fellow was.

I finished up attending to the bedding and set out to explore what evidence there was that I could find. Like the fox, voles do tend to be creatures of habit. They will find a place of their liking and return there to eat and forage. If that was what this fellow was about, well then, we should see what we should see.

Gatwick Park Days - *A Gardening Memoir*

It was another pleasant day in what had been a week of pleasant days. The grasscrete was trim and the embankment was smart as I made my way up to where the creature had been spotted. The beds had yet to receive their weekly tidy but were presentable and so I could afford to spend time on this investigation.

Voles have a preference to sit and eat in the same place, so piles of nibbled grass and stems may be left and that would decide the matter. Plants nibbled by water voles have a distinctive, angled cut at the ends. Their rounded, elongated droppings are notable also as tell-tale signs to identify water vole activity.

"Excuse me!" The voice had appeared as if from nowhere, else I was too absorbed in my reverie to notice her standing there on the grassed border. It was not unusual for me to proceed thus, with such a purposeful design I might well have been on a forced march! I have been so told on many an occasion.

"You're the gardener." It was a statement, not a question. I paused my stride and nodded across to her. I had not happened upon her before but, then, there were so many staff and our paths would not inevitably cross. As I approached her, she went on to comment upon the weather, the fine state of the grounds and then, straightway,

plunged into her purpose and intention in seeking me out.

Our encounter proceeded thus, by way of a long and protracted account, to explain why she had set out from the quiet but busy seclusion of her office to find me. Her daughter's wedding was fast approaching and she had noticed the fine clumps of Astilbe in full bloom along the banks. She was seeking my permission to cut some to use for the floral arrangements she had tasked herself to construct for the reception.

Now, both Aruncus and Astilbe are beautiful flowering plants that are often compared but, also, confused due to their very similar structure and habitat. There are, however, some very distinct differences between the two that set them apart. While both bear outstanding and striking floral plumes of downy and feathery form that make them so sought after, there are some subtle but quite notable differences in their overall appearance. Aruncus has a finer, wispy quality that gives it a more delicate, airy look. Astilbe, on the other hand, is more compact, more dense in appearance, and the flowers form thick and crowded clumps together in a huddle. The flowers that had caught her eye were not Astilbe but Aruncus.

Aruncus tends to have a more limited colour range, also,- from a creamy white to a creamy pinkish tone. Astilbe has a more diverse colour range. Aruncus typically grows taller, reaching heights of up to five feet and more. That is the most notable difference, perhaps. That in itself was the deciding factor, along with the shady habitat it had chosen and was faring so well in.

Aruncus is, by far, to be preferred of the two because of its fine and wispy plumes that sway so gracefully in the breeze, granting them a more delicate feel, certainly more suited to a floral display, and it was this, surely, that had caught her eye and taken her attention. I set out to explain this to her even though she would have none of it.

What had immediately caught my ear was her pronunciation of the word; I had thought better of it and chose not to remark upon this to her, however, in case of causing further offence. It is 'Astil-bee' and not 'Astilbe' which grants it more of a French articulation, stress, and intonation. It is the Latin pronunciation which is correct, in which every syllable is given equal emphasis. After all, French is only badly spoken Latin. Every French purist is now going to shoot me at dawn! I should care: I have heard it said the French consider English to be only badly spoken French!

In the matter of her identification of the plant, I attempted to persuade her otherwise but she would not be so persuaded from what she sincerely held to be correct. Her mind was settled; she sought only the permission to cut some stems for the bridal display. I was content to permit that, of course; it was growing there wild, in any case.

Having been granted permission, off she set on her way with a pace, her mission accomplished! Our encounter was at an end. I watched her as she walked back down the grasscrete to the rear service door where she disappeared from view. For a moment, briefly, I stood there, captured in a thrall as it were, as I pondered our exchange. Thereupon, my thoughts returned, once more, to the task in hand.

I reached the far end where the footpath bore left through the gate to the front of the building and, directly ahead of me, stood the summer house and the lattice-fenced 'secret garden'. Here, too, was the stepped footpath down to the boarded crossing that bridged the stream. I considered a moment, should I look there, but chose not to. It was, surely, not the sort of place that would accommodate a burrow.

I took the path to the left and proceeded through the gate. Here were the dogwood and, there, the stream hooked round the west wing to the front on its journey to meet the Mole. I began my investigation with impatience and enthusiasm to discover what might be found and to see what I might see.

The bank was more shallow here, not steep as it was further along as it approaches the drive, and just the place the creature might choose to sojourn for a morning feast. I scanned the slope carefully. There was no sign immediately visible to me to indicate any habitation. There were no burrows here to be seen I could discern.

The grassy bank slid straightway into the passage of the stream here as it hooked round into the straight channel it had carved out for itself along the front of the hospital, past the pair of Pedunculates that skirted the bend. The burrows, if there were any, would be found there, surely, but here was where the fellow had been sighted.

Then, I spied the mound! A pile of nibbled grass and stems, lying there in plain sight, presented itself. I had not seen but, now, I saw, and all were nibbled in that distinctive, angled cut at the ends. It was a vole she had seen! I set off down the stream to survey the bank where the stands of Willow Herb, Loosestrife and Meadowsweet grew. This was where I had dug out the smaller pond. There was the corrugated pipe which John had provided me and I had laid to channel the stream into the smaller pond; and, there, was the burrow! We had our very own 'Ratty' to grace our Willows!

Gatwick Park Days - *A Gardening Memoir*

The fellow had chosen a perfect spot for himself to settle in and make himself a home. The bank, protected by the overhang of tall vegetation was a perfect hide for his burrow. Some floral fronds of Aruncus stood here, also, and the thought of my earlier encounter returned to me. What if, I wondered; what if she, also, reported seeing a 'rat'! Such a confirmation from an independent witness might outweigh any of my protestations otherwise and that might easily imperil our very own 'Ratty' to his dire detriment.

Then I spied the elongated droppings that are so typical of his kind, no bigger than a sixpence. The sixpence is long gone! Perhaps, I should update that estimation of their size to a twenty pence piece. There were two separate deposits of the pellets on the bank, each on either side of the burrow. The fellow had been having his breakfast here before going out on his little jaunt to startle and cause such alarm and dismay! These were accompanied by another tidy pile of neat cut stems beside them to serve as yet further evidence.

The matter was settled then; at the very least, in my estimation it was so. The soil here was soft, too, and easily tunnelled, just as they prefer it to be. It was an idyllic and undisturbed earthy bank of the sort which the creature can burrow into with ease, with broad, wide margins and tall grasses and sedges for food and cover. All these were tell-tale signs of water vole activity and so I hoped the fellow would not be so badly misrepresented such that, falsely accused, they would feel the need and be impelled to summon the dreaded rodent catcher!

The water vole has such a positive affect on his habitat just by going about and pursuing his day to day activities. These all contribute to creating conditions ideal for other animals and plants to thrive in, - including that unwanted immigrant, the American Mink!

These are fierce and territorial creatures. They appear careless of whether they are seen, unlike the shy and secretive otter. Some escaped over the years from the farms where they were bred for their fur. Others were intentionally freed by activists campaigning to end the trade. I have come across one only once, as roadkill on the Longbridge roundabout.

Mink is smaller than the otter, a lithe creature with narrow snout and smaller face. This fellow was not bloodied, not at all, by his encounter. I had stopped off and shifted him into the verge rather than just leave him there at the roadside. I had visions of him slowly being pulverised into a homogeneous, unrecognisable accumulation by the relentless and unforgiving wheels, not even a carcass anymore but, featureless, spread by the butter knife of the tyre across the metalled surface of the road.

I confess I had mistaken him at first for an otter. He may well have been undertaking a passage, fraught with danger though it was, from across the Mole to our pond. That being the case, if so it was, our Mallards may well have lost their duck-chicks not to a Grand-daddy Pike at all, but to a Mink! Now, that was, indeed, a matter of some seriousness to consider.

I finished the day tidying up those borders and heard not a thing more about 'rats' from anyone I happened to encounter. The 'rats!' tale, so it appeared, had been stymied, then, with not another thing being said to me about it and my anxiety for our poor 'Ratty' subsided. The next few days passed and it was just a footnote on the clipboard of my memory.

Then, first thing in the morning at the end of the week, I glanced down the service road and spied the Rentokil van man exiting his vehicle with his bag of accoutrements bulging as he set out to lay his bait boxes in strategic places about the building. He stood there, I thought, like the exorcist at the door with that bag of his. I was bemused. The thought of my colleague, Roy, all those years ago, sprung to mind, also, and I went into action immediately to ascertain his business.

I greeted him suitably and amicably and drifted the conversation around to our 'Ratty'. No, no, he assured me with a ready smile, he was not about to lay traps down by the stream, only about the premises. I thanked him readily for the information and he set off again about his work, disappearing from my view through the rear service doors which flapped to a close behind him.

It is so very odd how occurrences recur, and continually so; perhaps, it is in the very order and nature of things that they should do and we draw attention to them only to design some order or reason into these haphazard events that, all strung together, we call life. Roy would be upset, I know, but not so upset, perhaps, as he might have been, as would I. Our 'Ratty' was safe - for a while, at least - unless he should chance to have an unfortunate encounter with some ruthless, immigrant predator...

GATWICK PARK DAYS: 12

The Great Flood

Flood information for the Povey Cross Stream at its entry point on the Gatwick Park site.

Historically, these Surrey-Sussex borders have ever been ill-renowned for their susceptibility to abrupt and extreme flooding. It has been quite typical that vulnerable and affected areas may suffer, in that manner, sudden and dramatic rises and falls in water levels, like the proverbial yoyo! At the Gatwick Park site, our grounds and their flood plain have suffered, very much so, in like fashion.

Flood plains act as holding areas for flood waters to prevent what would otherwise be a potentially catastrophic headlong rush into lower-lying areas. In our locale, this would be the Thames basin. London and its environs sit beneath this almost Damocletian threat and that is as ever it was. The combined efforts of a strong spring tide and prolonged heavy rain dumping it down upstream could spell almost certain disaster.

Gatwick Park Days - *A Gardening Memoir*

Even into the twentieth century, it was not uncommon for the river to overflow its bounds. My dear mother, growing up in Southwark, reported such happenings to me herself. This was why that engineering marvel, the Thames Barrier, was eventually constructed. The lack of a flood plain could well prove to be the proverbial straw that breaks the camel's back.

While yet maintaining the integrity of our flood plain, well designed drainage projects within its domain did prove most effective in much alleviating the effects upon the grounds themselves of such flooding and improving both the aspect and demean of the property. However, in recent times, these undertakings have been undermined and undone, their design and intention unable to forestall the engulfing effects of the extreme weather conditions we experienced.

Failure to attend to and maintain ditching appropriately or at all on adjacent properties also had its repercussions. There is a thought among some proponents of the environmental lobby to 'rewild' but this does have consequences. Failure to dredge waterways has impacts. The top flood meadow or callow was swamped three years in succession. Such failures of non-intervention in combination with other failures of intervention have exacerbated further the hazardous situation, although pressure put to bear by the previous

Gatwick Park Days - *A Gardening Memoir*

Hospital Manager did obtain effective dredging downstream of us on the adjacent property.

In recent times, whatever the cause and for whatever reason, over-winter flooding has worsened to such an extent that the floodwaters have attained heights unprecedented even for these grounds, not seen before, nor seen since. This all culminated in the case in point, and the point to which this tale is leading is the over-winter period of 2000. This particular event was quite unprecedented and came to be known by many as The Great Flood!

The Povey Cross Stream collects its catchment through the sprawling Charlwood farmland, gathering up the trickle of the Withey Brook upon its way. Culverted thence, it ploughs its subterranean course through Withey Meadows and out into the Gatwick Park grounds via its exit beneath the boundary fence. From here, the stream plies a way at the very edge of the steep embankment of the flood plain, through the very heart of the grounds, and tops up our pond in passing. It departs our grounds to wend its way, via the superstore, into the Mole.

In that winter of The Great Flood, the River Mole was already high from a swollen Gatwick Stream and was held back itself at the down water weir. Thus it was that the Povey Cross Stream found the exit of its flow into the swift traffic of the Mole's waters stopped. The waters backed up as though they were a jam of traffic upon a busy road. It is such a scenario at work that imperils the Thames basin: that very same feared combination of the downstream of the flow meeting an impenetrable surge into which it cannot escape.

The almost constant rainfall of recent days had swollen the water course to unprecedented levels. Such a sight it was that it might well have reassured Noah in his undertaking to construct the Ark; that it was not at all a vain endeavour but an undertaking of critical outcome! It was not just that the ground was sodden to the point it could swallow no more; rather, that it was just all too much at once and too much of a muchness, but that is the manner in which flooding so often occurs.

Water companies have reported aquifers to be at a record low and depleted level. That is not merely, nor necessarily, due to either less rainfall or greater demand but, also, to run-off trafficking precious rainwater into the drainage system of ditches, brooks and rivers – and flood plains. The precious rain is not being permitted to soak through to replenish the aquifers.

Those who promote housing development on local flood plains may take small comfort, therefore, from rash predictions of diminished rainfall here in the Southeast. Even were those predictions sound, still, that would not lessen at all the dangers of flooding in low lying and flood plain areas subject to such outcomes; and, in any case, flash flooding can affect anyone at any time.

If there is nowhere for the water to go, it will play havoc with any well-laid plan or scheme. Each garden paved over and patioed, tarmacked and turned over to the car; every infill housing development putting further strain upon an overburdened infrastructure and over-stretched resources: all this means less rainwater filtering through to aquifers and more risk of flooding through run-off.

It was one day at the beginning of December 2000; it had been yet another day, and just one more of many, of steady and unrelenting rain. Upon my journey to work early that morning, I had encountered the road flooded beneath many inches of water at the intersection of Woodroyd Avenue with Brighton Road. The footpath, too, was under water. There was no avoiding it: I would have to get my feet wet and traipse through it to make my way forward and get across to the other side!

Upon turning the corner and approaching the Longbridge roundabout, I found the ditches to be chock-full to the brim and the Mole already overflowing into Church Meadows, beyond the

Gatwick Park Days - *A Gardening Memoir*

tree-line opposite. Although not unprecedented, this was a rare enough event and never boded well; it was always a sign that our grounds would not be faring fine at all. The flood plain would be full and we would soon be suffering visibly, if not already, in that regard.

Traffic was reduced to a queue as it troughed and trundled through the sheet that trickled like a slick across the road, a treacherous gloss that skimmed its surface. A train of vehicles slowed and queued in turn, all upon their daily commute to Gatwick, to negotiate an onerous course through it, across the bridge, and onward toward the roundabout.

At first glance, the road more resembled a canal than a road! This was an unprecedented event in my own experience and, to my own knowledge, unheard of hitherto! The passing vehicles left a wash behind them, navigating almost like river craft. Their wake dribbled reluctantly through into the Texaco forecourt. A cashier's face peered nervously over the festive season advertising pasted to the plate glass window. A pictured speech bubble spoke: 'Should I call the lifeboat...?'

When I got into work, I found the flood plain a lake, the flow of the brook a mere undertow beneath, the top callow in flood and the rain

Gatwick Park Days - *A Gardening Memoir*

unrelenting. There was nothing very much would or could be accomplished on a day like this one. Overhead, a band of migrating Mallards, three in number, swung round, once, twice, before winging it out in the direction of the more sheltered Riverside ponds alongside the Gatwick Stream.

Along the rim of the bank, upstream of the drive, I had planted cuttings of Salicifolia which I had intended to drape down and tumble into the trickle below to provide a gay, white cloak of bloom. Hebe takes most readily and well, and did, but the trickle had become a torrent and the torrent a flood. The flow had risen to meet them and now stood at such a height that the slender swathes were actually swimming in the swirl of the current and the crossing I had constructed there was well and truly buried in the drink!.

The unremitting rain continued without letup and, later that day, the floodwaters were observed to be almost lapping the footpath that follows the brook round from the rear of the hospital. As the waters continued to rise and actually brink the footpath in part, the dire situation that threatened, very soon, came to the inevitable and unavoidable attention of those ensconced within the building.

No less a personage than the General Manager himself honoured us with his presence in the patient's area to observe the rising tide. Once the stream topped the footpath, the flood would surely hasten across the flat of the lawn toward the building! This frightening scenario was the prospect presented, which focussed minds and quickly became an obsession of those present witnessing the scene as a matter of urgency to deliberate and deal with.

This personage became so alarmed, in fact, and concerned that his trepidation quite overcame him and consumed him! The very thought of the possibility that the hospital might soon be engulfed and that he must stand by helplessly and witness it must have been daunting, indeed. His thoughts, likely, were a maelstrom that sucked him in to consider the potential outcomes and these would have been the prime consideration in his mind as he became particularly nervous and apprehensive and was seen to be waving his arms, pointing erratically this way and that.

The poor man hurled directives to the air, an appeal to heaven, perhaps, for aid. Then, he was heard to issue rapid instructions to those of his attendant lieutenants standing by him, shoulder to shoulder at his side! He was so agitated and concerned at what he deemed to be the impending threat to the hospital building that, in haste, without benefit of forethought, he passed the order for sandbags to be obtained.

Gatwick Park Days - *A Gardening Memoir*

It took all the powers of persuasion and gentle cajoling manner that the Works Manager could muster to convince him that, as the waters rose still higher and higher, it would take substantially ever greater volumes of water to push the level still higher and higher. Thus, it was only by this stolid, certain and persistent intervention that the command was rescinded. Even so, his alarm was extenuating and quite understandable in the circumstances.

The argument was, of course, perfectly valid. In addition, what no-one realised, nor I until I observed it for myself, was that, while we were all looking, in dismay, at the encroaching threat, the waters were already backing onto the recreation ground at the rear of the site, taking the load that threatened us with them.

Here, the stream exits from its culvert ahead of the boundary fence. The waters were an angry swirl of eddies and the culvert was submerged beneath. The water subsequently backed up, as I learned later, to invade properties on the small Withey Meadows estate beyond, flooding two homes.

The stream is culverted again beneath the drive. Here, the headroom is set low to accommodate the traffic of heavy goods vehicles that visit the hospital. Unfortunately, this creates a bottleneck and, once the water tops the head of the culvert, the floodwaters rise more readily because escape is obstructed. This has also undermined trees sited on the flood plain and, the previous year, brought down a white poplar.

The flood retreated dolefully, reluctantly, without complaint though, by May time, the flood basin was still sitting in water, extensively puddled and looking not at all what it would, normally, have looked. The plain would have dried out. I would have been able to run the tractor over for the first cut; but I wasn't able to do so for some weeks thereafter. Was this entirely due to the flood? It may well have been but, equally, could it be put down to the weight of the spoil, including some building material, being pushed onto the flood plain during prior construction work, squeezing the water table like a toothpaste tube, thus causing the puddling effect?

The Great Flood became a talking point of first resort in causerie and conversation. There was much excitement amongst the savants with wont to express their sage wisdom to any with pause to listen. There was much talk of the 'hundred-year flood'. This is a flood event that has, on average, a one in one-hundred chance of being equalled or exceeded in any given year. Victorian builders would never build in a flood plain. They had a great deal more sense, embanking the Thames and undertaking all the massive public sanitation works that transformed London. The boldness of the wise is in the recognition of their frailties.

"We've had our flood for the next 100 years, then," someone quipped in the restaurant next day. He was hastily corrected, that there could be another tomorrow; it was all to do with the odds. "I'm not a betting man!" the fellow retorted with a quick, wry smile and everyone sallied back with a banter of small talk and comment that merged incoherently into a mélange of concordant good humour.

This light-hearted persiflage and raillery, in ebb and flow predominated, back and forth, over an Admiral's Pie with parsley dressing, a Traditional Roast or two, or seconds of lemon meringue for many a week, and did not trail off, as all things eventually do, until longer days and fine summer suns encouraged talk of the 'hols' and far away places and exotic destinations. In the meantime, the restaurant was a buzz of banter and the more serious discussion which caused it.

"Someone's messing with the weather!" The assertion brought the lively conversation to a halt. "It's the chemtrails from the aircraft," the fellow went on. I interjected that these were vapour trails. The water vapour in the upper atmosphere condenses on the aircraft engines, vaporises and leaves the resultant trail. I had seen this on the high-flying Vulcan bombers back in the fifties. I

would always look out for the Vulcans and their distinctive v-wing outline on the way to school.

That brought to mind and caused me to mention when, working for Almans, a Redhill building company that held a contract to do 'Ministry Maintenance' as it was termed, I was called on to do maintenance at a tiny US Air Force station on the Golden Wheel Farm at Caterham where constant radio contact was kept with a B52 Bomber carrying a nuke ready to strike should duty call. This was at the height of the Cold War.

John, the Works Manager, retorted that it was good to hear it described as 'water vapour' as so many mistakenly call it steam! Heads turned at the adjacent table. "There's so many, though, all in straight lines." Then someone else chipped in that we are right by the airport and there are so many flights now so you might expect there to be, and they would be in straight lines. This damning logic did not deter others stirring up a veritable soup of pet theories as to what they were or what they could be!

"They're called contrails," an authoritative voice instructed. It was Bill. His jovial face beamed at us with an eager eye, just bursting to toss in his own two penn'orth. "They've been doing those rain-making exercises, experimenting with the weather for donkeys." His enthusiasm boiled almost to a whistle!

Gatwick Park Days - *A Gardening Memoir*

I jostled quickly for attention and enjoined that I remembered well going on a coach trip from Minehead as a child to visit the disaster that had befallen Lynmouth in North Devon. The Lyn had broken its banks and all but destroyed the village. That had been some five years previous and reconstruction was still proceeding then. There had been some talk of boffins and cloud seeding going on but this was a small-scale thing and could not have possibly caused the great depression that had loomed across the entire of the south-west peninsula and caused the rain to bucket down the way it did.

Bill's whistle blew! "They're not going to admit to anything like that, now, are they? You know what they say about ripples making waves!" The cat thrown in amongst the pigeons, his eyes twinkled with glee.

"Someone's messing with the weather!" The voice was insistent. It was the same fellow again, making the same assertion, and that brought the entire conversation full circle. "It's the chemtrails from the aircraft!"

Amidst a brief shock of silence, someone else piped up, "You mean jet-wash, don't you? You always seem to get a whiff of it when it's going to rain. They're not supposed to but they jettison fuel to gain height." Another corrected that the trails were just cirrus streaks. Bill paused, as if to see where the conversation would lead. Was he egging the two on, as if just to see how far he could stretch their bounds of belief?

No such luck! The melange of chatter was going nowhere. It had been brewing up like a great depression, from table to table in an engulfing tide, but amounted to only a damp squib on a sodden bonfire night. The lively conversation dwindled and fizzled out into engaging table talk on such matters of great portent but small outcome as the lucky dip for the upcoming lottery draw!

Was that a shrug of reluctant acceptance? Bill snuck back into the remains of his Beef Wellington with an enthusiastic gusto, savouring every last portion that remained.

GATWICK PARK DAYS: 13

The Final Curtain

I commenced these accounts, putting pen to paper, with reports of my brother suffering a cerebral accident that confined him to a wheelchair, unable to communicate, but eating at last! It takes a little jog sometimes, perhaps, to commence a course of action; although, this was more a substantial jog than most and more a substantial undertaking.

Making a record or keeping a log may put thoughts in order to keep them on a more level par and that was much needed. The care of my dear mother fell to me and this I undertook to my best ability.

We religiously visited her stricken son and, upon returning from one such visit, found the house to have been burgled. Her room, her personal space, had been rummaged through. There was nothing to be found; she had nothing of value but that of sentiment to her, but that was not the point. She had been violated and sentiment, in any case, is beyond price. So cruel and merciless an action it is to defile cherished memories.

Gatwick Park Days - *A Gardening Memoir*

They must have been keeping a watch, observing our movements, our comings and goings, and seized upon the opportunity. She received a letter from victim support but the police never paid her a call. Burglaries are an ordeal but a common enough occurrence! They have matters of more urgent calling to attend to, perhaps.

I undertook the upkeep of my mother's garden and made it a joy for her for a while, at least. A bird table was added at the front, along with a sundial I picked up from a sale of work and fitted to a hexagonal plinth constructed from concrete by means of shuttering to fashion it. To finish it off, it was given a coat of masonry paint two-toned, like a lighthouse, and this even afforded a favourable comment from a near neighbour upon the 'jazzy' garden feature.

I will conclude now with news of her sad passing and lay my pen to rest, but not before adding some additional notes and observations. A garden, like a home, is a life's work in progress and gardening, like housework, is never done, never complete or completed and never a topic at a loss to talk about and share.

NOTES AND ANECDOTES

The Order of the Spade

Quite taken aback, I felt humbled, surprised, unworthy. Someone had, without my knowledge or telling, kindly nominated me for the BUPA Ambassador Award! Amongst seven other more worthy members of staff, more deserving than me by far, my name had also been selected.

The award had just been newly launched at Gatwick Park and, spending the majority of my time out in the grounds, I was not aware of its introduction until being told that I was one of the nominees. We all assembled at a presentation ceremony attended by the Recognition Schemes Manager at which we received our certificates from the hospital General Manager.

As an extra touch – the icing on the cake, if you will – they presented me with a spade! This was the very spade that was used to 'break the earth' at a ceremony to plant daffodils on the approach to East Surrey Hospital, Redhill where our new partner hospital, Redwood, had recently opened. This was only a token, I realise, but a most kind thought I think all the same.

Garden Features

It is always a good idea to add features of interest to a garden. A hedge placed strategically may effectively break up an otherwise bleak aspect. Who cannot but admire the patchwork fields of England? A feature may then be added to that feature. A stile, perhaps, might add interest to the hedge? The notion quite took my fancy and so I set my mind to it with a vigour.

The aspect of the open field was, indeed, a bleak one that, so partitioned by a hedge, if planted with thoughtful care and due attention, might ably serve to draw the eye, as on a canvas, from one feature of the landscape to another such that all come together to complete the whole. The thought of it was tantalising certainly. A hedge is quickly populated with fauna and flora and so encourages an abundant variety of life.

The far field was perfect for the purpose of the project, or so I judged, and I spent my spare moments digging and preparing the ground to accommodate the planting. The budget was always a concern and this persuaded me to lay the proposed hedge with heel cuttings of hawthorn and elder, of which there were plenty growing about, and these would fill out and soon provide bulk and bloom to it, and so it was soon done.

The hedge provided a continuous barrier, from the pond precincts right up to the solid wall of Leylandii along the boundary but, here, a break was provided to enable passage of the tractor to mow. Halfway along the unbroken line, or thereabouts, a gap was left to accommodate the stile, and this object was promptly and readily achieved, using repurposed fence posts and offcut timber so to construct it.

One of the consultants, soon after, suggested I lay down duckboards to make a boardwalk beyond the stream to navigate the flood plain when damp and boggy. We had pallets discarded in the skip on occasion which could be knocked together and they would have served most ably but I would have needed quite a number and more besides to complete a walk of any useful extent. The practicalities of it also concerned me. It was an undertaking I ever kept in mind but never, in the end, pursued.

Over the years, as timber presented itself, if it was suitable and sound, many crossings were added to bridge the stream and provide interest. When two scaffold tubes of suitable length became available, a bridge of suitable structure was constructed to support the weight of the tractor and this enabled access to the pond precincts to mow, accomplishing the task more readily and in a trice!

Gatwick Park Days - *A Gardening Memoir*

A perfect feature for a garden is, of course, a bird table! Watching the birds fly down to feed and squabble over the scraps is ever a most admirable thing to take the time to stop and stare at. I made one for my mother's garden and set it in the centre of the front lawn but, as she pointed out to me afterward, I should have set it further back to better enable viewing their comings and goings from within the house, through the window.

She was ever the sensible observer; the obvious is not always so readily or immediately discerned. My attention, my focus, had been upon the aspect and balance of the setting; hers was upon the purpose and strategy of having a bird table, which was to view the toings and froings of the avian traffic to the table!

A bird table, given a strategic position, becomes a focus for the eye whilst remaining a part of the general landscape of the setting. It gives a human aspect to the outlook. Such a table may readily be knocked together out of a discarded pallet or other timber retrieved from a builder's skip. Just ask, and it will usually be the case that the builder will only be too glad of an offer for it to be removed.

Seating is always a requirement for a garden. A rustic bench formed with tree stumps and plank is a simple and basic addition which sits naturally into its environs. One such was added to the pond precincts, beneath the towering overhang of the Pedunculates, from where to observe the navigations of the pond's residents across the still water. The attraction quickly drew the attention of the curious and the adventurous to venture down there from the viewing area upon the promenade to savour its delights. Here, many a summer night was spent in vigil with a hot flask for company!

Such simple pastimes are not just for children. They are a hunger for the heart and a solitude for the soul, to mend the mind and find a calm to restore and repair. A space of time there spent, within those quiet precincts, in order to reflect upon the muddles that beset us is surely a solace to favourably compare with anything a healing retreat may tempt us with. Now, that is a thought to satisfy any tormented soul and set aside those weighty burdens that travail, even though for just a brief while snatched from the turmoil of the working day.

'Upcycling' and Repurposing

This is only what everyone used to do but they didn't call it that then. It wasn't done to 'save the planet' but because it made sound economic sense to make ends meet. Hence all the weekly 'sales of work' and jumble sales we used to see, especially before the advent of so-called charity shops, which now seem to accept only the highest quality of donation! From darning socks to unthreading threadbare woollens to reknit anew into some fresh attire, this is what everyone did, just to get by, and many a tight budget was balanced thereby to the great relief of many a Micawber or Coolidge!

You might think the odd scraps of wood that come your way, that you may stumble upon or which may be offered to you, would restrict you or limit you in your choice of project but this 'ain't necessarily so' as the song goes. Being so confined, the project will often design itself, forcing you to be resourceful, innovative and providing much satisfaction at the end of it to have put such discarded odds and ends together to some good use.

If you're doing some tree work, a lopping may catch your eye. Features may stand out that resemble some shape or form. Turn your hand to it and see what can be made of it. Even the humble pebble or stone upon the beach may, likewise, grab your attention and infuse your imagination to create something quite unique.

Pause before discarding something. Set it aside and ask of yourself, instead, what could be made of it to bring it to life or bring it back to life. Refurbish an old pot. Knock together an eye-catching container. Every such addition adds character to a garden and makes it a talking point. A lick of paint; a coat of varnish: both may revitalise and make as good as new.

Ever think twice before discarding something as outdated, outmoded or redundant in favour of the new and novel which may, given the careful thought it deserves, only be a novelty you will quickly regret. All too often, the clarion call of 'out with the old' and 'in with the new' is adopted to the great detriment of what, after all said and done, did actually possess an originality and a character unique to it and quite irreplaceable.

This very thing occurred when the hospital had to adopt the new corporate branding! It was all a big thing at the time, yet the old signage did possess that very individuality and uniqueness its very own. That was of no consideration at all, of course. It was all a matter of 'Ring out the old' and 'Ring in the new'!

Listen to your Garden

'Listen to your garden'. That may sound an odd thing to say but, let it speak to you, and it will tell you what to do. Even then, having proceeded with an undertaking, adjustments to that design will become clear to you. There will be fine-tuning; additions and subtractions will be made until everything falls into place.

Gatwick Park Days - *A Gardening Memoir*

Some people like to start out with a design already in place and they will suggest this to you. That's fine, too. In fact, you may receive an abundance of advice in your endeavours and it is always good, most certainly polite, to keep an open ear and listen. It is rewarding and profitable to gain the lesson of experience that others have been taught or been forced to learn. Ultimately, however, you will find that what works best is what works best for you.

Brian, whose mantle I took on and whose good company I shared in the grounds for some six fine summers long, maintained a reservoir in his hanging baskets, and this worked very well for him, and yet I had always been told it would encourage disease. When roots sit in water too long, they swell. This can cause rot and mildew; it also keeps the roots from absorbing nutrients. His baskets, however, were always in glorious bloom, producing an abundance of flower.

It is always important to keep the soil moist and bear in mind that rain will not penetrate the canopy of leaf and bloom readily. Also, the tender roots have no access to a sub-strata of soil as do plants in the ground and the basket is, quite literally, hung out to dry in the in the sun, day long, throughout the summer months.

Always water whatever the weather and do offer a

supply of water at the same time each day. I used to cycle in on weekends to check them for that very reason. This consistency helps plants adjust and helps prevent stress. A watering first thing is usually best. An early drink will set them up for the day. It also keeps the plants from sunscald – a splash of water may act as a magnifying glass to burn into the leaves in the mid-day sun.

You can't make a plant do what it doesn't want to do. If a plant is not comfortable in its situation, it will not grow well, or not at all. Mother Nature always knows best. When planting, do firm in well as it is important that the roots make intimate contact with the soil, sufficient to make a purchase. Old-time gardeners would check the work of their young wards by giving the plant a gentle tug. If it pulled up readily, it was not a proper job done well. Then, do stamp in with boot or by hand to make it so.

A rule of green thumb with a lawn is to keep it cut and keep it watered to encourage the fine grasses. Cut out the offending intruder in your lawn with an old dinner knife through the root. A pinch of salt dropped into the hollow will finish it off.

Use the same blade to weed out the crevices between the paving slabs. It works as well, if not better, than a weed-killer and, needless to add, is no hazard to the user. I remember well, years

Gatwick Park Days - *A Gardening Memoir*

previous, as Groundsman at the Comprehensive in Horley, the big issue Dioxins caused with their associated serious health issues. Slabs kept swept will not readily permit a seed to germinate in any case. An American cousin daily sweeps her yard, as a chore to undertake even when it does not appear necessary to do so.

An old-time gardener would use a soft broom to gently brush the lawn back into shape to give it a good appearance rather than cut when wet and shock the grass. Anecdotally, one such old-time gardener, so I learned, who was in the habit of presenting the lady of the house with a posy of violets, would scent them, unbeknown to her, with a splash of Devon Violets and she would ever make admiring comments, complementing him on their 'wondrous' bouquet! If ever she suspected his deception, she never once made comment to chastise or embarrass him.

Take cuttings to increase your plant stock. Many plants root readily, some more readily than others. You may take a cutting from the stem. Cut just below the leaf bud, at an angle to it, and plant straightway in compost. Repair the stem you have cut from by cutting back to just above the next leaf bud in the manner as you would when pruning.

Taking a heel cutting is often much easier and more successful. This is known as a 'bit of old and a bit of new'. Select a nice-looking side shoot and gently snap it in a downward motion to tear it from the stem. You will be left with the side shoot – a bit of new – and a bit of the stem – a bit of old – attached to it. Again, plant as soon as you may.

Salicifolia, which has been given prior mention, is a Hebe. The Hebes come originally from New Zealand. They number in the hundred in their variety and are distinguished by their segmented stems, each of which may readily strike to grow a new plant.

Do dead-head to promote more flower but do keep seed for next season. When the flower finishes, a pod forms which contains the seed. The seed heads will become crisp. Pluck them, either individually or with their stalks attached, and keep them in an old envelope or bag to store, writing on it what seeds they are. Choose a dry day for this and keep them in a dry place.

Some ripe seed heads will burst into the bag. Some, like Pansies, will hold forth their seeds. Depending on the plant, the process of pollination will provide the seed plant with different qualities to that of the parent. If the parent is a F1 Hybrid, it will not 'breed true' but bear characteristics from either of the parent plants that produced them.

Do introduce new stock to retain vigour and variation and not be reliant entirely on your own seed. You may find otherwise but it is my experience that - in those plant species, such as Petunia or Begonia, and others, which produce a multiplicity of colours - the eventual outcome will be a generation of all white blooms.

Of Remedies and the Remarkable

Wash off aphids and spittle fly with a hose. With the former, you may also gently wipe the fresh shoots which they always go for toward their tip with your hand to remove them. You may even see the industrious ant toing and froing to 'milk' their aphid charges of the honeydew they collect!

Mildew can be treated with Bordeaux Mixture. This may be readily made up from a mix of copper sulphate and lime of equal parts, ten grammes each in one litre of water, mixed well together. Spray or brush onto the infestation. Remove the cause, usually unkempt terrain, by tidying and aerating the soil around the base. Hard hose the residue mildew from the trunk.

The Crab Tree in my mother's garden was treated in this fashion. This particular tree had the most peculiar formations on its trunk that gave the appearance of loppings having been taken from it, but it was nothing of the sort. The evidence that presented itself was not of loppings but of galls.

A gall is an abnormal growth stimulated under the influence of an infestation of some sort, bacterial or fungal. The invading organisms promote uncontrolled cell division in the host tree which then produces the gall by penetrating the cells and causing them to proliferate and enlarge abnormally. The infesting organisms adapt the environment of the host to cater for their own needs. It is the botanical equivalent of a cancerous tumour. Is there more than a parallel here for what prompts cell division to cause such tumours?

There is a large variety of galls. They may appear on any part of the tree. Insect infestation may also prompt their formation. There are burls or crown galls. Burls are effectively benign tree tumours. Burls were once sought after and prized by furniture makers. Imagine! Remarkable is life. Miracles and marvels abound all about us for those with eyes to see. Just take the time to stop and stare.

The joy and wonder of life is that we are, forever, seekers. Everywhere, all around us, there are miracles in abundance to see;- unfathomable, splendorous to behold. We have only to open our eyes to recognise them.

Gatwick Park Days - *A Gardening Memoir*

PHOTOGRAPHIC ILLUSTRATIONS

Gatwick Park Days - *A Gardening Memoir*

You don't know what you don't know.
The unknown is only discoverable.
Live in dreams but not delusion;
Live in hope but not expectation.

Gatwick Park Days - *A Gardening Memoir*

The field outcrop.

The flood plain in flood.

Gatwick Park Days - *A Gardening Memoir*

The Duck House on the bank upon completion.

The Duck House settled on its raised piles in the small pond.

Gatwick Park Days - *A Gardening Memoir*

The hedge laid with heel cuttings.

The hedge with stile constructed as a feature to provide interest.

Gatwick Park Days - *A Gardening Memoir*

The One Life Award.

The Award Ceremony.

Gatwick Park Days - *A Gardening Memoir*

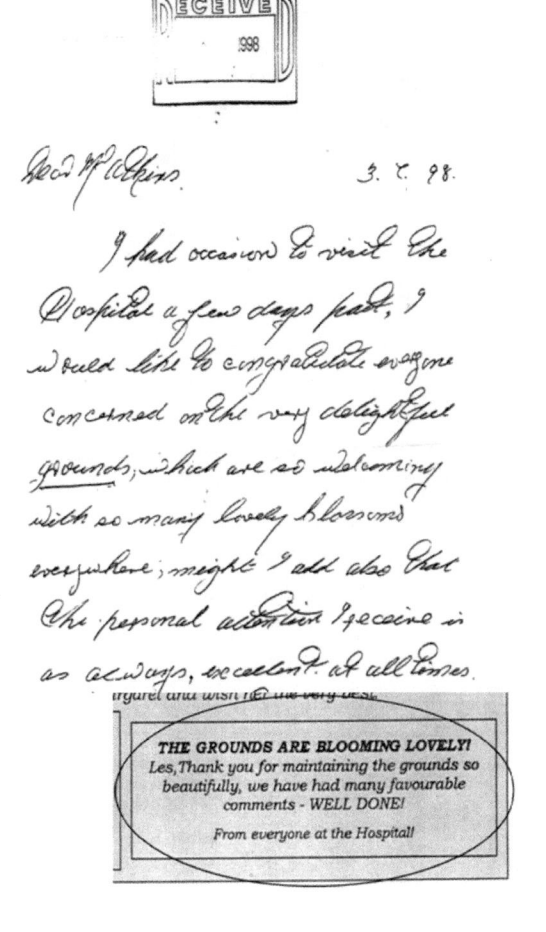

[RECEIVED stamp, 1998]

Dear Mr Atkins.   3. 7. 98.

I had occasion to visit the Hospital a few days past, I would like to congratulate everyone concerned on the very delightful grounds, which are so welcoming with so many lovely blossoms everywhere; might I add also that the personal attention I receive is as always, excellent at all times.

THE GROUNDS ARE BLOOMING LOVELY!
Les, Thank you for maintaining the grounds so beautifully, we have had many favourable comments - WELL DONE!

From everyone at the Hospital!

Comments of appreciation, unsolicited, by letter and by word of mouth

Gatwick Park Days - *A Gardening Memoir*

The floating island from the promenade.

The floating island from the far bank.

Gatwick Park Days - *A Gardening Memoir*

At the top of the drive - 'Ring out the old…'

And - 'Ring in the new…'

Gatwick Park Days - *A Gardening Memoir*

Crossing to the rustic bench in the pond precincts.

The bird table in the 'secret garden'.

Gatwick Park Days - *A Gardening Memoir*

Bringing on the seedlings and bedding.

The grasscrete up to the 'secret garden'.

Gatwick Park Days - *A Gardening Memoir*

The viewing area from the pond precincts.

The pond precincts with the pair of Pedunculates.

Gatwick Park Days - *A Gardening Memoir*

Carp water – "The pair of Pedunculates that skirted the bend."

Carp water – The stream, culverted beneath the drive.

The Moorhen – "a loud and abrupt hiss would come from across the fringes of the pond."

The Mallard – "a devoted but quite careless parent…"

Gatwick Park Days - *A Gardening Memoir*

The Salicifolia – "which I had intended to drape down and tumble into the trickle below."

Top – Viewed from the drive. Bottom – Viewed toward the drive.

Gatwick Park Days - *A Gardening Memoir*

The front entrance.

January snowscape.

Gatwick Park Days - *A Gardening Memoir*

The "steps cut into the steep bank of the brook."

"…the stout boards that girded its width."

Gatwick Park Days - *A Gardening Memoir*

Stands of Purple Loosestrife and the Aruncus, "its fine and wispy plumes that sway so gracefully in the breeze"

The crossing that was well and truly buried in the drink!

Gatwick Park Days - *A Gardening Memoir*

"My eyes perceived a sable form lying prostrate upon a soft bed of pine droppings."

"He stood there, calm as day, standing over something."

Gatwick Park Days - *A Gardening Memoir*

"A bridge of suitable structure was constructed to support the weight of the tractor."

"Many crossings were added to bridge the stream and provide interest."

Gatwick Park Days - *A Gardening Memoir*

From this, to this – "the project will design itself…"

"…forcing you to be resourceful and providing much satisfaction at the end of it."

Gatwick Park Days - *A Gardening Memoir*

"Refurbish an old pot…"

"Knock together an eye-catching container…"

Gatwick Park Days - *A Gardening Memoir*

"Features may stand out that resemble some shape or form."

"The humble pebble or stone on the beach may, likewise, grab your attention …"

Gatwick Park Days - *A Gardening Memoir*

" Take cuttings to increase your plant stock."

"The evidence that presented itself was not of loppings but of galls."

Printed in Great Britain
by Amazon